HERBERT LOCKYER

THE *Gospel* IN THE PENTATEUCH

I0808014

WHITAKER
HOUSE

All Scripture quotations are taken from the King James Version of the Holy Bible.

The Gospel in the Pentateuch

ISBN: 978-1-62911-831-4
eBook ISBN: 978-1-62911-832-1
Printed in the United States of America
© 1939, 2017 by Ardis A. Lockyer

Whitaker House
1030 Hunt Valley Circle
New Kensington, PA 15068
www.whitakerhouse.com

Library of Congress Cataloging-in-Publication Data

Names: Lockyer, Herbert, author.
Title: The Gospel in the Pentateuch / by Herbert Lockyer.
Description: New Kensington, PA : Whitaker House, 2017. | Originally published: Chicago : The Bible institute colportage ass'n, c1939.
Identifiers: LCCN 2017009004 (print) | LCCN 2017010065 (ebook) | ISBN 9781629118314 (trade pbk. : alk. paper) | ISBN 9781629118321 (ebook)
Subjects: LCSH: Bible. Pentateuch—Study and teaching.
Classification: LCC BS1227 .L6 2017 (print) | LCC BS1227 (ebook) | DDC 222/.106—dc23
LC record available at https://lccn.loc.gov/2017009004

No part of this book may be reproduced or transmitted in any form or by any means, electronic or mechanical—including photocopying, recording, or by any information storage and retrieval system—without permission in writing from the publisher. Please direct your inquiries to permissionseditor@whitakerhouse.com.

2 3 4 5 6 7 8 9 10 11 24 23 22 21 20 19 18 17

CONTENTS

PREFACE

In his most helpful work on the Pentateuch, S. Ridout makes the following introductory remarks, which we take the liberty of using to introduce this simple study.

> There can be no doubt that we are justified in taking the first five books of the Bible as forming a group by themselves.
>
> The division of the Old Testament Scriptures into the Law, the Prophets (former and latter), and the Hagiographa, or Kethubhim, (the Sacred Writings) has always been recognized and is the division mentioned by our Lord Himself when He said: "That all things must be fulfilled, which were written in the law of Moses, and in the prophets, and in the psalms, concerning me"

(Luke 24:44); and the "psalms" included the other poetical books.

There can be no question that these first five books were written by Moses....Our Lord evidently considered the first five book of the Bible as the inspired product of Moses: "For [Moses] wrote of me. But if ye believe not his writings, how shall ye believe my words" (John 5:47).

We could not think of putting the Pentateuch in any other but its present place, at the beginning of the entire Book of inspiration. Morally, historically, and doctrinally, it forms the introduction to all that comes after. If, for instance, we plunged into the history of Israel in Joshua, we would be ignorant of the antecedents of the nation, of God's ways with them, and of the reasons which had led Him to take them up in distinction from all other nations. Similarly, if we placed the Pentateuch at the close of the Old Testament, we would find that the preceding books of the Prophets and Psalms were largely inexplicable.

The Pentateuch is an essential introduction to the entire Word of God. It opens that which is afterwards unopened, and ever leads us on in hope of a consummation which, though distant, is certain.

Not only is the Pentateuch an introduction to the Scriptures as a whole, but we may say it is the model upon which the entire Word of God is written.[1]

---

1. Samuel Ridout, *The Pentateuch* (New York: Bible Truth Library, 1919).

With these weighty words of Mr. Ridout before us, we are prepared to enter upon a somewhat general survey of the books of Moses.

It is needless to say that much help has been derived from various Bible study books, and grateful acknowledgment is made for all of these contributions.

In the preparation of the following chapters, we have had in mind the Christian worker who has little opportunity for more extensive study.

The questionnaire at the conclusion of each book will, it is hoped, assist leaders in Bible school work, group classes, etc.

—Herbert Lockyer

1

THE ROMANCE OF THE BIBLE

The Bible is the masterpiece of the divine Mind. For over eighteen centuries it has existed as we now have it. Whatever indication of human arrangement there may be about it, it bears the stamp of divine inspiration. At the back of all human construction there is the hand of God. The Bible is not an arsenal of texts for preachers to choose from; it is a divine textbook.

In this meditation it will be our endeavor to present a bird's eye view of the contents of God's incomparable Word.

THE OLD TESTAMENT

In this first part of the Bible, the theme of redemption is in its early, incomplete, and typical form. Two stages are presented, namely:

The Introduction: Genesis to Deuteronomy—5 books.

The Development: Joshua to Malachi—34 books.

1. The Historical Books

The origin and establishment of the Israelite nation: Genesis to Ruth.

The development and fortunes of the kingdom: 1 Samuel to Esther.

The record of the origin of the plan of redemption, and the chosen nation to whom it was committed by God through Moses for themselves and the world, is given in the Pentateuch. Each of the five books presents a different phase:

Genesis—Origin of creation and the nation.

Exodus—Commandments and ordinances given to the nation.

Leviticus—Way of access to and worship of God.

Numbers—Organization of the nation.

Deuteronomy—Preparation of the nation for the land.

The word *Pentateuch* means "five books," and these books are known as "the Law."

In the development of the national life of Israel, we find the people under a *theocracy*. *Theos* means "God."

In *Joshua*, the nation is in the land.

In *Judges*, the nation is tried and fails.

In *Ruth*, we see the origin of the messianic king.

From *theocracy*, the nation passes to *monarchy*. Visible kings now preside over the affairs of the people. Six books are taken up with this phase of the nation's development:

1 and 2 Samuel—Deliverance of the people. Their religious reformation. The Davidic covenant.

1 and 2 Kings—The civil history of the nation to the captivity. Failure of the monarchy.

1 and 2 Chronicles—Religious history of the nation to the decree of Cyrus.

First, we see the kingdom united under Saul, David, and Solomon. Then the kingdom is divided—Israel with ten tribes and Shechem as its capital; Judah with two tribes and Jerusalem as its center. The kingdom being united again is the theme of the prophets.

After the captivities we have the *dependency*. The restoration to the land under the rule of Gentiles covers three books:

Ezra—Return of the remnant and rebuilding of the temple.

Nehemiah—Rebuilding of the walls of Jerusalem. Renewal of covenant.

Esther—God's providential care of His people in the dispersion.

We can apportion the ministry of the prophets to the Historical Portion in this fashion:

The preparation of the people for the coming of the Messiah is contained in sixteen books of the Bible:

1. Seven prophets seek to save Israel and Judah from Assyria—*Joel, Amos, Isaiah, Micah, Obadiah, Jonah,* and *Hosea.*
2. Four prophets seek to save Judah from Babylon—*Nahum, Habakkuk, Zephaniah,* and *Jeremiah.*

3. Two prophets seek to save a remnant and to prepare them for restoration—*Ezekiel* and *Daniel*.
4. Three prophets of the restoration guide the remnant and prepare them for the coming of the Messiah—*Haggai, Zechariah,* and *Malachi*.

2. *The Poetical Books*

This section is distinctively experimental in character. The development of the religious life of the people forms the burden of these six books. Each book is taken up with some phase of experimental godliness. Thus are portrayed the characteristics of the King's elect.

A. Didactic: Practical Religious Life

Job—The suffering of the righteous. The elect are here instructed in the death of self.

Proverbs—Obedience to God in daily life. The divine guidance and daily conduct of the elect are here in view. This book gives a series of practical and sententious counsels. "Wisdom" and "wise" are its keynotes.

Ecclesiastes—Vanity of worldliness. The elect are here taught the emptiness of earthly gain. "Vanity" and "under the sun" are its pervading keynotes.

B. Lyric: Devotional Religious Life

The Psalms—Religious feelings. The varying experiences of the elect are here clothed in the language of prayer and promise. The keynotes are "blessed" and "praise."

The Song of Solomon—The love of the soul for God. The union and communion of the elect with the King is the spiritual message of this book.

Lamentations—The Giver of national blessings. Because of its likeness to poetry, we include Jeremiah's work under this section. Here God is seen as the Friend of the elect.

3. The Prophetical Books

This section is usually separated into two divisions, namely:

A. Major Prophets

Each prophet, it will be found, has his peculiar and distinctive title or description of the King, whose coming they all proclaim:

Isaiah—The King who comes to subdue rebellion and establish His authority. Isaiah's keynote is "glory."

Jeremiah—Jehovah of Hosts who comes to punish sin and teach the righteous. "Evil" is this prophet's keynote.

Ezekiel—The Lord God comes for chastisement. He punishes His covenant people for their unfaithfulness to covenant obligations.

Daniel—The Ancient of Days, the God of heaven, casts down earthly thrones. "Kingdom" is Daniel's keynote.

B. Minor Prophets

So called because smaller in compass.

Hosea—Israel is the unfaithful wife. The King is *Ishi*, "my husband." "Return" is the keynote.

Joel—Jehovah plagues the land, then restores it. "The land" is Joel's keynote.

Amos—Adonai-Jehovah, the God of Hosts, punishes and then uplifts a sinful people.

Obadiah—The cruel brother of Israel is rebuked. "Esau" is the keynote.

The four succeeding prophets point to the instruments that the King will use at His coming:

Jonah—Type of unfaithful ministry. Jehovah-Elohim chastens. Keynote of the book is "arise."

Micah—The remnant is brought low, yet preserved by God's grace and faithfulness. Keynote is "the remnant."

Nahum—This prophet predicts the overthrow and destruction of the proud, imperial city of Nineveh. Keynote is "no more."

Habakkuk—The personal antichrist. Double keynote, "the wicked (one)" and "love to Him."

The remaining group foretells the issue of the King's coming, with immediate reference to contemporaneous events. Here events are antitypes.

Zephaniah—The appearing of "The King of Israel, Jehovah." The great tribulation. Keynote, "the day of wrath."

Haggai—Return from Babylonian Captivity. The temple rebuilt. The appearance of "the Desire of all Nations." Points forward to the glorious and permanent reestablishment. Keynote, "Jehovah's house."

Zechariah—The King, Jehovah of Hosts, is in the midst. Predictions are not limited to time or age. Keynote, "the city rebuilt."

Malachi—The King as Jehovah of Hosts is again prominent. Foretells the renewal of the national covenant with Israel. Keynote, "return."

THE INTER-TESTAMENT PERIOD

The blank page in our Bibles between the Old and New Testaments represents a period of some four hundred years. There is no biblical account of what transpired during these four centuries. Secular history, however, fills in the blank. A most interesting and concise account of this period is given by Dr. C. I. Scofield in the *Scofield Reference Bible,* under the title of "From Malachi to Matthew." As a background to the New Testament, one could also read *The Four Hundred Silent Years,* by Dr. H. A. Ironside.

Politically, the fortunes of the Palestinian Jews followed the history of the Gentile world empire foretold by Daniel (see Daniel 2:7), with one exception—the Maccabean revolt.

Religiously, the history of the Jews during the long period from Malachi to Christ followed, and the outer ceremonial, the high-priestly office, the temple worship, and the course of the troublesome political history are of scant interest.

During this period there arose the two great sects known in the gospel narratives as Pharisees and Sadducees. Under their hands traditions accumulated—traditions which Christ tried hard to destroy as He exercised His ministry. As the drooping moss, growing in different parts of Florida, covers all trees and ultimately destroys their beauty and life, so the moss of tradition obscured the law, and Jesus had to spend much of His time clearing away such parasitical growth.

THE NEW TESTAMENT

The second part of our Bible is called "New," seeing that it introduces a New Dispensation. B.C. (Before Christ) covers the Old Testament. We now come to A.D. (The Year of Our Lord).

The books of the New Testament can be conveniently gathered into seven distinct groups:

1. First Group–The Christ of the Gospels

The first three gospels are known as the Synoptic Gospels, seeing as they largely adopt the same viewpoint:

Matthew—Christ the King. Keynote, "kingdom." Our Lord's genealogy is traced from Abraham. Symbol, the lion.

Mark—Christ the Servant. Keynote, "immediately," an appropriate word for a Servant of God and man. Symbol, the ox.

Luke—Christ the Man. Keynote, "the Son of Man." This gospel provides a full account of His human origin. Genealogy goes back to Adam. Symbol, the Man.

John—Christ as God. Keynote, "I AM." Deity is the dominant feature in John. Symbol, the eagle.

2. Second Group–The Christian Church

Acts—The history of the church's foundation. Keynote, "the Holy Ghost."

Romans—The message of the church. Keynotes, "righteousness" and "faith."

I Corinthians—The membership of the church, with its privileges and responsibilities. Keynote, "called to be saints."

2 Corinthians—The ministry of the church. Keynote, "ministry."

3. *Third Group–The Christian Believer*

Galatians—The liberty of the believer. Keynotes, "bondage" and "liberty."

Ephesians—The standing and status of the believer. Keynote, "in Christ."

Philippians—The progress and development of the believer. Keynote, "more."

Colossians—The life of the believer. Keynotes, "risen" and "hid."

4. *Fourth Group–The Christian Hope*

1 Thessalonians—The second coming of Christ in relation to the church. Keynote, "coming."

2 Thessalonians—The second coming of Christ in relation to the World. Keynote, "He shall come."

5. *Fifth Group–The Christian Pastor*

1 Timothy—The pastor set forth as ruler. Keynote, "charge."

2 Timothy—The pastor as worker or servant. Keynote, "endure."

Titus—The pastor as instructor. Keynote, "sound doctrine."

Philemon—The pastor as a spiritual man. Keynote, "brother." He is responsible for a rich effusion of Christian love and sympathy.

6. Sixth Group—The Christian Profession

Hebrews—The Christian profession contrasted with the Mosaic economy. Keynote, "better."

James—The Christian profession in relation to practical morality. Keynote, "works."

1 Peter—The Christian profession in relation to a persecuting world. Keynote, "suffering."

2 Peter—The Christian profession in relation to false teachers. Keynote, "knowledge."

7. Seventh Group—The Christian Faith

1 John—The Christian faith: Live it! Keynote, "we have."

2 John—The Christian faith: Guard it! Keynote, "His doctrine."

3 John—The Christian faith: Further it! Keynote, "the truth."

Jude—The Christian faith: Hold fast to it! Keynote, "kept."

Revelation—The Christian faith: Its glorious consummation. Keynotes, "amen" and "come quickly." This climactic book of Scripture combines the subjects of 1 and 2 Thessalonians. Glory, grace, and government are Dr. G. Campbell Morgan's suggestions for its convenient divisions: glory (chapter 1); grace (chapters 2–3); government (chapters 4–22).

QUESTIONS FOR REVIEW

1. What is the Bible?
2. For how many centuries has the Bible existed as we have it today?
3. How many principal divisions in the Old Testament? Name them.
4. What is the great theme of the Old Testament in typical form, and through what nation was it revealed by God?
5. What were the three forms of government employed in the Old Testament?
6. What were the divisions of the kingdom of Israel after the reign of Solomon? How many tribes in each division?
7. What prophets sought to prepare the people for the coming of the Messiah?
8. What are the two divisions of the poetical books? Name the three books in each division.
9. What are the two great divisions of the prophetic books? Give the names of the books under each division.
10. About how many years intervened between the Old and New Testaments?
11. How many groups of books in the New Testament? Name them and give the keynote of each book.

2

GENESIS: THE BOOK OF BEGINNINGS

INTRODUCTION

It is important to commence our study at Genesis, not only because it is the first book of the Bible, although such is the proper way of obtaining a right viewpoint of truth, but because the Bible contains a succession of revelations, progressively unfolded, and Genesis is the first of these revelations.

Further, Genesis gives us a synoptic preface to the entire Bible. It is the seed-plot of the Bible. The germ or beginning of all truth is within this wonderful book. Genesis is the foundation upon which the entire revelation rests; the root out of which the rest grows. Truths found here are developed in successive ages.

And, as the name suggests, it is a book of beginnings. Final revelation is not here. Dr. A. T. Pierson has urged us to watch "the law of first mention." Genesis gives us the first mention of many truths, and is therefore the most indispensable of all books. It is the foundation, the beginning, and the anticipated explanation of all others.

ITS TITLE

The Jews called it *Bereshith,* the Hebrew word for the first three words of Genesis 1:1—"*In the beginning.*" The Greek translators named it *Genesis,* meaning "origination" or "production," seeing that it is a book of origins or beginnings. Genesis records the beginning of all things except God, who had no beginning. Creation, man, Sabbath, marriage, sin, sacrifice, nations, governments, and so on, all are introduced therein. As yet there was no church, temple, or synagogue. The head of the family was ruler, priest, and prophet.

ITS AUTHOR

Old and New Testament writers ascribe the authorship of Genesis to Moses. Its Mosaic authorship was unanimously accepted by the Jews. The highest authority concerning the book as a work of Moses is the Lord Jesus Christ Himself. And His acceptance of the Mosaic authorship not only of Genesis but of the Pentateuch is a sufficient reason why we should do likewise. (See Matthew 8:4; Mark 7:10; Luke 24:27; John 1:45.)

Modernism, however, acting upon supposed internal evidence, has assumed that the different names used of God indicate that various authors wrote the book. The theory of a composite authorship made up of editors or redactors spoken of as J. E. D. P., which stand for the Jehovist, the Elohist, the Deuteronomist, and the Priestly Code, has been set forth. Redaction means to arrange in systematic order. Such an effort to explain the authorship of Genesis, however, is nonsensical, for surely Moses could employ different names for God as other Scripture writers have done.

We contend that Moses either obtained authentic records, selected his material, and then wrote the book under the guidance of the Holy Spirit, or that he received a direct revelation from God of all that is written therein.

As the art of writing was known at a very early period, the transmission of historical events during the first few centuries was possible. There is nothing against the idea of events being transmitted as family heirlooms from Adam to Methuselah and Noah; from Noah to Abram, Abram to Isaac, Isaac to Jacob, Jacob to Joseph. Adam lived until Methuselah was 243 years old. Methuselah lived until the flood and conversed with Noah. Noah lived until Abram was fifty years old.

In the last verse of Genesis we find the body of Joseph in a coffin. Was anything else deposited therein? Were ancient records buried with that body and later discovered by Moses when he removed it from Egypt?

It would seem as if passages like Exodus 24:12 and Acts 7:37–38 leave no doubt as to the origin of the book. It was born on Mount Sinai. An old Rabbi has it that "Jehovah dictated to Moses the contents of the book during the first forty days that he was allowed to have communion with Him, and that when he came down from the Mount he committed the truth to writing."[2]

2. Attributed to Rabbi Moses Ben Nachman in Thomas Hartwell Horne, *Introduction to the Critical Study and Knowledge of the Holy Scriptures* (Philadelphia: J. Whetham & Son, 1841), 204.

As Daniel and John received apocalyptic visions, so Moses had the past laid out before him, and being a master in the art of penmanship, he was able to set forth an orderly composition of the highest kind.

The only answer or explanation of many things within the book is that it was a divine revelation. Take, for example, the record of creation where fifteen scientific facts are stated in their order and accurate relation.

Such scientific knowledge was beyond the range of ancient philosophy. In fact, several announcements within the creation narrative have only been made understandable by modern discoveries. How came Moses to be so accurate? There is only one tenable explanation: Genesis is a divine revelation.

And his equipment as a writer is guaranteed by the fact that Moses was learned in all the wisdom of Egypt, spent forty years in Midian where he was taught the deep things of God, and was a man of God, a prophet, and a servant of the Lord. (See Deuteronomy 33:1; 34:10–12; Acts 7:22; Hebrews 11:26).

ITS CHRONOLOGY

Genesis covers a period of some 2,400 years. The first part of the book, namely, chapters 1–11, represents some 2,000 years; while the last section, chapters 12–50, is devoted to the history of 400 years.

ITS KEYNOTE

This is struck in Genesis 1:1—"*In the beginning God.*" Not chance, not law, not matter or force, but God. God has stamped

His name and sovereignty upon the very forehead of the book. "God first" in creation, redemption, providence, and personal experience gives the right attitude in thought and action. Is this our keynote—God first in everything?

The conspicuous message of Genesis is that of divine sovereignty. Everything is traced back to God, seeing that He is all in all. He dominates the scene.

Is it creation? God created.

Is it man? The Lord God formed him.

Is it man's destruction by the flood? The Lord God sent rain from heaven.

Is Noah preserved? The Lord shut him in.

Did Abram come up from Ur? God called him.

Was Jacob's nature changed? God wrestled with him.

Did Joseph become ruler? God preserved him.

The book is likewise eloquent with the message of divine grace and love. God is revealed not as a mere tribal deity, but the same in both testaments. Then the provision of altars proclaims the truth of divine holiness. God hates sin and can only meet the sinner on the basis of the shed blood.

ITS PURPOSE

It has been said, "The roots of all subsequent revelation are planted deep in Genesis and whoever would truly comprehend that revelation must begin here."[3]

3. C. I. Scofield, *The Scofield Study Bible* (New York: Oxford University Press, 1996 [1909]), 1.

The primary purpose of the book was not to give us a scientific account of creation, but to show how God prepared the Hebrew nation to be His peculiar inheritance and the depository of the plan of redemption. It was written to define the place to be occupied by Israel among the nations of the earth, and how, in response to the divine call and in accordance with the purpose of God, she gradually emerged from among the other nations with a separate and distinct existence as the people of Jehovah. As the result of this, the book reveals how the theocratic institutions founded by Moses were rendered possible and necessary. Such, we take it, is the key-structure of the book.

A broader purpose of the book is to outline the preparation of the earth for man, and the place he should occupy on the earth under the sky. Genesis was not written to tell man all about the heavens, but how he could go to heaven.

ITS SUBJECTS

What august themes the book introduces to us!

God is revealed as Creator, Redeemer, and Provider.

Man's entrance, fall, and redemption are also given.

Sin's nature and development are revealed, as unbelief and rebellion prevail.

Satan's subtlety, work, and defeat are proclaimed.

Christ as the coming Deliverer is forecast.

Genesis gives us a general history of mankind and a particular history of the patriarchs. And such a history is the oldest and most trustworthy in the world.

ITS CHARACTERISTICS

A right understanding of Genesis means a right understanding of the rest of the Bible. It is too late in our day to reject its claims, seeing that such are being daily authenticated by the discovery of tablets and monuments.

1. A Book of Beginnings

Genesis states the beginning of everything except God. It does not prove but assumes His existence. What cannot be traced to its beginnings in this marvelous book? The universe, life, man, sin, sorrow, death, redemption, Sabbath, covenants, arts, trades, marriage, family, nations, governments, music, literature, agriculture, mechanics, cities, and languages—all these are here traced to the fountainhead.

2. A Book of Types

Andrew Juke's "Types of Genesis" is a valuable handbook to have, if the typical nature of the book is being studied. Said Christ of Genesis, "*Moses…wrote of me*" (John 5:46), therefore He is the key of all. In Adam, the man; Jacob, the servant; Isaac, the son; and Joseph, the ruler, we have clearly defined types of Christ.

Types of the church can be traced in Eve, Rebecca, Rachael, and Asenath. The believer is typified in characters like Abel, Enoch, Noah, and Abraham.

3. A Book of Contrasts

Some of the contrasts of the book are very marked. The two natures—Cain and Abel; the worldly and the godly—Lamech and Seth; faith and sight—Abraham and Lot; law and grace—Ishmael and Isaac, Hagar and Sarah.

Attention has been drawn to the contrast between Adam and Christ.

Adam	*Christ*
The first Adam	The last Adam
The image of God	The very image of God
Of the earth	Of heaven
A living soul	A life-giving spirit
Lord over creation	Lord over all
Overcome	Overcomer
Yielded to the flesh	Yielded to the Spirit
Excused himself when justly accused	Silent when unjustly accused
Fell; bore judgment	Victorious; abolished judgment

One is also struck with the contrast of Genesis, the first book of the Bible, and Revelation, the last book. Several writers have expounded this feature. Here is the excellent explanation given by the Rev. J. Sidlow Baxter:

> Note the *similarities* between Genesis and the Apocalypse. In both we have a new beginning and a new order. In both we have the tree of life, the river, the bride, the walk of God with men; and in both paradises we have the same moral and spiritual ideals. God has never abandoned the Eden ideal for man; and although in the end

the garden has given place to the city, the Eden ideal of holiness finally triumphs. In Genesis we are given a mere glimpse of what went *before* the new beginning; then we are told how the new beginning took place; and then there follows a good deal of what happened *afterwards*. In the Apocalypse we have the same kind of construction, but in the inverse order. First, and mainly, we are shown what *leads* to the new genesis; then we are told how the new beginning takes place; and finally, in the closing chapter, we are given a glimpse of what lies beyond it.

Mark the *contrasts* between the one book and the other. In Genesis we see the first paradise *closed* (3:23); in Revelation we see the new paradise *opened* (21:25). In Genesis we see *dis*possession through human sin (3:24); in Revelation we see *re*possession through divine grace (21:24). In Genesis we see the "curse" imposed (3:17); in Revelation we see the "curse" removed (22:3). In Genesis we see access to the tree of life disinherited in Adam (3:24); in Revelation we see access to the tree of life reinherited in Christ (22:14). In Genesis we see the beginning of sorrow and death (3:16–19); in Revelation we read, "*There shall be no more death, neither sorrow*" (21:4). In Genesis we are shown a garden into which defilement entered (3:6, 7); in Revelation we are shown a city of which it is written: "*There shall in no wise enter into it anything that defileth*" (21:27). In Genesis we see man's dominion broken in the fall of the first man, Adam (3:19); in Revelation we see man's dominion restored in the rule of the new Man, Christ (22:5). In Genesis we see the evil triumph of the serpent (3:13); in Revelation we see the ultimate triumph of the Lamb (20:10; 22:3). In Genesis we see the walk of God with man interrupted (3:8–10); in Revelation we see the walk of God with man resumed, and hear a great voice from heaven saying, "*Behold, the tabernacle of God is with men, and he will dwell with them*" (21:3).[4]

4. A Book of Historic Realities

Modernism has a great deal to say about the beautiful myths and stories of Genesis; even that Adam and Eve were not historical personages. Well, genealogies bulk largely in the book, and myths do not possess a lineage. In fact, these genealogies form a framework for the history and reveal the plan of the book as we shall later show. Biographies and historic events are faithfully recorded and are heavy with the providence of God.

5. A Book of Theophanies

Theophanies or pre-incarnate appearings of our Lord in human form are another unique feature of this book. Any reliable Bible dictionary gives a full list of these appearances.

6. A Book of Covenants

Promises or covenants are another noticeable characteristic of Genesis. Particular promises are given in passages like 3:15; 8:21–22; 9:11–17; 12:1–3, 7; 13:14–17; 15:18; 17:3–8. Four dispensations can be traced:

1. Innocence: Creation to the fall (1:26–2:25)

---

4. J. Sidlow Baxter, *Explore the Book* (Grand Rapids: Zondervan, 1966), 25–27.

2. Conscience: The fall to the flood (3:1–8:22)
3. Government: The flood to Babel (9:1–11:32)
4. Promise: Babel to the Exodus (12:1–Exodus 19:8)

There is an old Latin proverb that translated reads, "Distinguish the dispensations and the scriptures will harmonize."

7. Its Authenticity

The findings of higher criticism are summed up by George Adams Smith in the statement: "The framework [of the first eleven chapters of Genesis] is woven from the raw material of myth and legend."[5] The pick and shovel, however, are causing the modernists to revise their theories. During the last few years an immense treasure of ancient inscriptions has been unearthed and deciphered. Discoveries in Babylonia (Babel) have given the most powerful support to the biblical accounts of creation, the deluge, and the dispersion at the tower of Babel. Genesis cannot be dispensed with, seeing that it contains the most reliable history of the world for the first two millennia.

We surely can detect Satan's purpose to discredit, if possible, the opening chapters of the book, seeing that they record his blasting of man's innocence and his consequent need of redemption, a work involving Satan's overthrow. And anyone doubting the reliability of Genesis is usually at variance with the claims of other parts of Scripture to inspiration. Containing, then, the

5. George Adams Smith, *Modern Criticism and the Preaching of the Old Testament: Eight Lectures on the Lyman Beecher Foundation*, Yale University (New York: A. C. Armstrong and Son, 1902), 92.

only authentic history, we see that Genesis bears the stamp of divine origin, whether it be pre-adamite, primeval, or patriarchal.

ITS RELATION TO THE PENTATEUCH

At this point it is necessary to say something concerning the relationship of Genesis to the rest of the Pentateuch. The first five books of the Bible, known as the Books of Moses, or the Law of Moses, are called "The Pentateuch," a title meaning the "five books" or "fivefold books." *Pente* means "five"; *teuchos* means "book." The Jews called these books "The five-fifths of the Law," or simply "the fifths." It is probable that originally the whole was one, divided into five sections, each section having as its title its first word or words.

Taken together, these five books constitute a progressive spiritual unity, setting forth in their main features, what has been described as "the order of the experience of the people of God in all ages."[6] Each book, then, is a part of another. For example, in Genesis we have election; in Exodus, redemption; in Leviticus, communion; in Numbers, direction; in Deuteronomy, instruction. Surely our pilgrim progress is indicated therein. Elected by God, redeemed by blood, brought into holy fellowship, led along our pilgrim way, taught the deep things of God. Other phases of such a relationship will appear for consideration as we approach the other Pentateuchal books. The following outline by J. Sidlow Baxter, proving that these five parts are full of purpose and progress, and contain the Bible in miniature, will suffice at this point:[7]

6. C.I. Scofield, *The Scofield Reference Bible* (New York: Oxford University Press, 2005 [1909]), xxii.

7. Adapted from J. Sidlow Baxter, *Explore the Book* (Grand Rapids: Zondervan, 1960).

The Human Side

Genesis	Ruin through the sin of man.
Exodus	Redemption by blood and power.
Leviticus	Communion on the ground of atonement.
Numbers	Direction—guidance—by the will of God.
Deuteronomy	Destination through the faithfulness of God.

The Divine Side

Genesis	Divine sovereignty in election and predestination.
Exodus	Divine power in redemption and emancipation.
Leviticus	Divine holiness in separation and sanctification.
Numbers	Divine goodness and severity in judging and preserving.
Deuteronomy	Divine faithfulness in discipline and destination.

The Pentateuch also gives us a five-fold portrait of Moses:

In Genesis, he is the sacred historian.

In Exodus, he is the long-expected deliverer of Israel.

In Leviticus, he is the law-giver.

In Numbers, he is the leader of the hosts of God.

In Deuteronomy, he is the prophet, forerunner of the Christ.

ITS PRESENT VALUE

There is not only the book's historical value, but a spiritual value which faith willingly accepts. When the events and histories are prayerfully studied, one guiding principle seems to stand out, namely, the setting aside of the flesh for the Spirit. Isaac displaces Ishmael; Jacob supersedes Esau. Character study is most helpful to faith. For example, the three great periods of Abraham's life are his awakening, his discipline, and his perfecting. Jacob's stages of growth are likewise marked: supplanter, servant, saint, seer.

The value of Genesis is also seen in its revelation of the unity, personality, and omnipotence of God. Here we see Him as the living, loving, and gracious One, approachable to man but unapproachable by man without the shedding of blood.

ITS ANALYSIS

Beginning with the primeval dispensation in Eden and ending with the patriarchal dispensation in Egypt, this book has been outlined in several useful ways.

Outline of the Generations

Owing to the recurrence of the phrase, "*These are the generations,*" or "*The book of the generations,*" it would seem that the most natural division is that which revolves around this characteristic term. Used some eleven times, it describes the genealogical character of its history, and divides the book into twelve parts.

Such a method supports the contention that Moses, under the guidance of the Holy Spirit, wrote the book.

Analyzing the book upon this plan, we have the following analysis:

1. The Introduction (1–2:3): Restorative and creative work of God during the first week.
2. The Generations of the Heavens and the Earth (2:4–4:26): Adam, Eve, serpent, first descendants of first parents.
3. The Generations of Adam (5–6:8): Seth, development of evil, deluge.
4. The Generations of Noah (6:9–9:29): Ark, new covenant of human government.
5. The Generations of Noah's Sons (10–11:9): Shem, Ham, Japheth; failure at Babel.
6. The Generations of Shem (11:10–26): Shows ancestry of Abraham.
7. The Generations of Terah (11:27–32): The call and varied experiences of Abraham.
8. The Generations of Ishmael (25:12–18): The bondwoman's son.
9. The Generations of Isaac (25:19–35:29): Whole of his history is a type of Christ.
10. The Generations of Esau (36:1–8): His prosperity and love of riches.

11. The Generations of Esau's sons (36:9–43): Record of dukes.
12. The Generations of Jacob (37:1–50:26): The twelve sons and tribes.

Primeval, that is, belonging to the first ages (chapters 1–11).

Patriarchal, a patriarch being one who governs his family by paternal right (chapters 12–50).

Outline of Generation, Degeneration, and Regeneration

Dr. G. Campbell Morgan's analysis of the book is also helpful:

1. Generation (1–2)

Of the material to man (1–2:3); origin, ruin, revealed cosmogony

Of man, as to nature and office (2:4–25); created, crowned, conditioned, completed

2. Degeneration (3–11)

Of the individual (3)

Of the family (4–5)

Of society (6)

Of the nations (11)

3. Regeneration (12–50)

Of the individuals (12–35:21)

Of the family (35:22–38)

Of society (39–50:21)

Of a nation (50:22–26)

Outline of the Patriarchs

Being a book of outstanding personages, they can be made to act as landmarks and assist memory in a general outline of the book.

1. Adam (1–5)
2. Noah (6–11)
3. Abraham (12–26)
4. Isaac (25–27)
5. Jacob (28–36)
6. Joseph (37–50)

Outline of the Beginnings

Taking the title of the book as given by the Jews, we can treat Genesis as a book of beginnings or origins:

1. The Beginning of the Material Universe (1:1–25)
2. The Beginning of the Human Race (1:26–2)
3. The Beginning of Human Sin (3:1–7)
4. The Beginning of the Revelation of Redemption (3:8–24)
5. The Beginning of Human Family Life (4:1–15)
6. The Beginning of Godless Civilizations (4:16–9)
7. The Beginning of the Nations of the World (10)
8. The Beginning of the Confusion of Languages (11)
9. The Beginning of the Hebrew Race (12–50)

Outline by Primeval and Patriarchal History

Another simple and easily-remembered arrangement is that of primeval and patriarchal history:

1. *The History of the Human Race—Primeval (1–11)*

From the creation to the fall (1–3)

Creation and God's week of work (1–2:3)

The garden and the probation of man (2:4–25)

The serpent and the fall of Adam and Eve (3)

From the fall to the flood (4–8:14)

Cain and Abel and their offerings (4:1–16)

The genealogies of Cain and Seth (4:17–5:32)

The great apostasy and divine judgment (6–8:14)

From the flood to Babel (8:15–11:9)

The new world and the new covenants (8:15–9:29)

The posterity of Noah's three sons (10)

The confederacy and confusion at Babylon (11:1–9)

2. *The History of the Hebrew Race—Patriarchal (11–50)*

The history of Abraham (11:10–25:10). A call supernatural in manner.

The history of Isaac (21–27). A birth supernatural in nature.

The history of Jacob (25:19–50). A care supernatural in exercise.

The history of Joseph (30:22–50). A control supernatural in direction.

It will be noticed that several portions overlap. One cannot say with precision that one portion ends here and another commences there.

Outline by Four Sections

The book may be studied also in the following sections:

1. Introduction (1:1–3:24)

The origin of the plan of redemption; of man, sin and salvation. This provides a foundation for the future revelation. The fact of the creation of man is given in the first chapter, and the mode of his creation in the second. God's rest is a type and a prophecy. Creation rest (Genesis 2:2); redemption rest (Hebrews 1:3); eternal rest (1 Corinthians 15:24–28). Corresponding to this there is the believer's two-fold rest—soul rest (Matthew 11:26–29) and eternal rest (Hebrews 4:9). Note the protoevangelium, or first gospel, in Genesis 3:15, in which are foreshadowed the incarnation of the Deliverer, His sufferings, and His ultimate victory.

2. First Section (4:1–11:9)

The covenant of works, the promise of the Seed, and the sacrifice for sin. Failure is seen in Cain, the Cainites, and the descendants of Noah. Note the revelation that God gives of Himself in connection with the flood and the renewal of the covenant with Noah.

3. Second Section (11:10–21:18)

The origin of the elect nation and the better covenant. The call and career of Abraham. The destruction of Sodom and Gomorrah, and the renewal of the covenant of grace with Isaac and Jacob. Note the increasing clearness of the revelation of the divine purpose.

4. Third Section (21:19–36:43)

Histories of Isaac and Jacob. The danger of relapse and the power of faith. The discipline and training of Jacob.

5. Fourth Section (37:1–50:26)

The career of Joseph. The preparation for the future. The chosen family dwelling in Goshen to be developed into a nation and fitted to receive the Law.

QUESTIONS FOR REVIEW

1. Why is Genesis named "The seed-plot of the Bible"?
2. What is the meaning of the title of the book?
3. Give proof of its Mosaic authorship.
4. What were the writer's sources of information?
5. How many years are covered by the book?
6. Does Genesis have a keynote adaptable to life? What?
7. Outline its dominant messages.
8. State the purpose of the book.
9. Suggest its characteristic features.
10. 10. How would you prove its authenticity?

11. What does the term "Pentateuch" mean?
12. Does Genesis bear any relation to the other Pentateuchal books?
13. Has the book any present-day value? If so, explain.
14. Analyze the book.

3

EXODUS: THE BOOK OF REDEMPTION

INTRODUCTION

The Book of Exodus records the greatest migration on record. Over two million souls on the march! Surely history has no spectacle to equal this. Exodus presents a great forward movement in the work of redemption. "While Genesis is a history of the old creation of nature, Exodus is an account of the new creation of redeeming grace."[8]

ITS TITLE

In the Hebrew Bible the Jews call this book *Ve-elleh Shemoth*, meaning "These are the names," a title founded upon the opening

8. Matthew Henry, quoted in James Macgregor, *Exodus* (Edinburgh: T. & T. Clark, 1889), 13.

words of chapter 1:1. The LXX (Septuagint) version gives "Exodus" as meaning "a going out" or "a departure" because of its subject, namely, the departure or going forth of the Israelites out of Egypt. This same Greek word is used three times in the New Testament: Hebrews 11:22, where it describes the exit of Israel; Luke 9:31, where it refers to the atoning death of Christ; and 2 Peter 1:15, where the apostle uses it to describe his own death.

In classic works, the word "Exodus" possesses a twofold significance:

1. The idea of an army or array marching out. Exodus 13:18 bears this meaning: "*Israel went up harnessed out of the land of Egypt,*" or arrayed in a triumphal march.
2. It denotes a festive procession, e. g., a bride's departure from her father's house to her destined home. Israel was to remember that the "Exodus" was the day of her spousal. (See Jeremiah 2:2; Hosea 2:15.)

Later on, Exodus was spoken of as the "Book of Damages," because of the legalistic aspect of the latter part of the book.

ITS AUTHOR

There is no reason to doubt the Mosaic authorship of Exodus. Christ and His apostles accepted such. (See Mark 12:26; Luke 16:29.) The Pentateuch was Moses to them, and what was Moses to them may well be Moses to us.

It is evident that the writer of the book was an eyewitness, and records events within his own personal knowledge, and was thoroughly acquainted with the life and customs of Egypt and of the Sinai Peninsula.

Historical revelation commenced with the call of Moses in Exodus 3. He was then eighty years of age as he took up his pen to record the communication of a divine revelation.

ITS SCOPE

The book covers some two hundred years, from the descent into Egypt to the creation of the tabernacle. Acts 7:15–44 supplies us with a full historical reference. Containing forty chapters, a number corresponding to the number of years spent in the wilderness, the book constitutes a real "pilgrim's progress."

Twelve chapters are allotted to life in Egypt—a people crushed and crying.

Six chapters with their march to Sinai—a people freed, led, and fed.

Twenty-two chapters to the giving of the Law, the making of the covenant, and the setting up of the tabernacle—a people taught and established.

ITS KEYNOTE

"Passover." The idea of passing over occurs in different connections, namely:

1. The blood-sprinkled houses (12:13).
2. The firstborn of Jehovah (13:12).
3. The Red Sea (15:16).
4. The River Jordan (Joshua 3:14).

All these suggest great Christian truths. In chapter 12:27 there is an inspired interpretation of the Passover and therefore of the Lord's Supper. It includes:

The doom of death.

The sacrifice of an innocent victim.

The reception of those who believe.

The destruction of those who disobey.

It has been pointed out that "passover" is a feminine word and is used, not in the sense of "passing by" but of "hovering over," as a mother bird hovers over her young. *"I will pass over* [hover over] *you"* (12:13). Protection, then, is the inner meaning of the word.

ITS KEY VERSES

Three verses, forming a triad, can be chosen.

3:8 gives God's declaration. There is oppression.

12:23 states the accomplishment of God's plan. There is redemption.

19:4–6 indicates the consequent character of the people. There is obedience.

The book, then, is one of redemption. (See 6:6; 15:13.) In Luke 9:31 redemptive work is called a *decease* or *exodus*. Bring my people out of Egypt! And here the drama of redemption begins in earnest and it is wrought out on a colossal scale. Deliverance is the end and purpose of revelation.

ITS PURPOSE

A careful study of the book brings a two-fold purpose to view, namely:

1. To show that the promises made to Abraham were fulfilled; that his descendants, after centuries of oppression in Egypt, would be brought out triumphantly. Count the adverbs, adjectives, and nouns descriptive of the promise in Genesis 15:12–16, and see how it was fulfilled.
2. To describe the giving of the law and the purpose of redemption. The history of the people is a parable of redemption, illustrating deliverance from spiritual bondage. The incidents recorded throw light on the way of salvation. (See Luke 2:38; John 3:14.)

ITS LESSONS

1. God. Jehovah is supreme, ruling in Egypt and Master of nature. He is faithful to His choice and will not draw back. He is holy and requires obedience to His will. He gives food, help, guidance, and so on, when these are needed.
2. Redemption by blood and power. The story of Exodus is repeated in every redeemed soul. There must be a "going out" in order that there may be a "going in." The worldly Egypt must be left behind.
3. Instruction follows deliverance; therefore, at Sinai, laws were given to them for the regulation of life and worship.
4. The giving of the moral law was followed by the giving of the ceremonial or typical law which sets forth in

figure Christ and His redeeming work. It is a revelation of grace.

ITS RELATION TO THE PENTATEUCH

Exodus is the second book of the Pentateuch or Law, and continues the history of Genesis, although there is a silence of some one hundred years between the end of Genesis and the beginning of Exodus. Instead of the opening word, "*Now,*" we can use the conjunction, "And." A conjunction is a word joining words or sentences together, such as "fire and water." These conjunctions in the opening sentences of each book prove the unity of the Pentateuch. (See Exodus 1:1; Leviticus 1:1; Numbers 1:1; Deuteronomy 1:1, with Numbers 36:13.)

The events recorded in Exodus are referred to in the rest of the books of the Bible. To understand the rest of the Bible, a knowledge of Exodus is necessary. Genesis left Israel as a family or house. Exodus leaves Israel as a nation, organized under chiefs with a settled form of worship and law. God's entrance into the tabernacle completes the theocracy. The Patriarchal Dispensation ends and the Legal Dispensation begins.

Other national and spiritual connections should be noted:

In Genesis the earth rises out of darkness into light. In Exodus Israel emerges out of the darkness of Egyptian bondage into light and liberty.

The beginning of Genesis speaks of those struggles which preceded the re-creation of the earth for occupancy by man. Before their exodus, Israel's condition was likewise "*without form, and void*" (Genesis 1:2).

At the creation the earth was brought forth out of water on the face of which the Spirit moved. It is not without meaning that the great leader of Israel, its mediator and lawgiver, Moses, was drawn out of water from whence he received his name.

Also Israel, whose children had been merged in water, rose to new life out of the waters of the Red Sea, over which the Spirit brooded in the cloud, and they were baptized into Moses in the cloud and in the sea.

In Genesis the earth is born by the Spirit out of the water. In Exodus Israel is born anew by the Spirit out of the water.

The book has also a vital connection with the rest of the Pentateuch.

Genesis is the book of divine call: grace.

Exodus is the book of deliverance: redemption.

Leviticus is the book of holiness: sanctification.

Numbers is the book of jealousy: direction.

Deuteronomy is the book of love: instruction.

THE TYPES IN EXODUS

Exodus contains a store of information for the scholar and is a source of inspiration for the believer. The fortunes of Israel prefigure the slavery of sin, backslidings, discipline, and deliverances in all Christian experiences. The tabernacle and its ritual is a rich mine of types and metaphors of Christ and His salvation.

Seeing that Exodus is a book of types, it may be well to devote a page or two to a consideration of the book's value as related to these types.

1. Moses

The divinely chosen leader of Israel, David Livingstone's favorite, is a conspicuous type of the Lord Jesus Christ. His life, as we know, is divided into three sections:

1. From his birth until the flight into Midian: 40 years. There he is shown as *Somebody*.
2. From his flight into Midian to the Exodus: 40 years. Moses there learned that he was *Nobody*.
3. From Exodus to his own exodus: 40 years. Then to him God was *Everybody*.

Christ can thus be seen in the perils of His infancy, the voluntary surrender of royalty, training in solitude, and leadership of the people out of captivity.

Dr. C. I. Scofield's suggestive outline is worth recording:

> Moses is a type of Christ as the Deliverer (Isa. 61:1; Luke 4:18; 2 Cor. 1:10; 1 Thess. 1:10).
>
> 1. A divinely chosen deliverer (Exod. 3:7–10; Acts 7:25; John 3:16).
>
> 2. Rejected by Israel, he turns to the Gentiles (Exod. 2:11–16; Acts 7:25; 18:5, 6; 28:17–28).
>
> 3. During his rejection he gains a Gentile bride (Exod. 2:16–21; Matt. 12:14-21; 2 Cor. 11:2; Eph. 5:30–32).
>
> 4. Afterward he again appears as Israel's deliverer and is accepted (Exod. 4:29–31; Rom. 11:24–26; Acts 15:14–17).
>
> 5. Officially, Moses typifies Christ as prophet (Acts 3:22, 23); advocate (Exod. 32:31–35; 1 John 2:1, 2);

intercessor (Exod. 17:1–6; Heb. 7:25); leader or king (Deut. 33:4, 5; Isa. 55:4; Heb. 2:10); while, in relation to the house of God, he is in contrast with Christ. Moses was faithful as a servant over another's house; Christ as a Son over His own house (Heb. 3:5, 6).[9]

2. *Redemption*

This blood-red book is a valuable handbook on redemption. The blood of the lamb saved Israel from the plague of death. The power of God saved them from the dominion of Pharaoh. The believer is redeemed by the blood of Christ from the guilt and penalty of sin (see 1 Peter 1:18), and delivered by the Spirit from sin's power and tyranny (see Romans 8:2; Ephesians 2:1–2). The whole set-up of the tabernacle typifies the work of redemption and communion.

Redemption is wholly of God (see Exodus 3:7, 8; John 3:16):

1. through a Person (see Exodus 2:2; John 3:17);
2. by blood (see Exodus 12:13, 23, 27; 1 Peter 1:18);
3. by power (see Exodus 6:6; 13:14; Romans 3:24; 8:2; Isaiah 59:20).

3. *The Lord Jesus Christ*

What a great time Christ must have had when He came to expound the things in Exodus concerning Himself! Why, the book takes on a new luster when we try to see His face in all we read!

---

9. C. I. Scofield, "Exodus 2," *Scofield Reference Notes, 1917 Edition,* available at biblestudytools.com.

Take the first period: Israel in Egypt (chapters 1–12).

It is surely Christ that we see in the child born and plotted against in infancy, but preserved from that death to which other Hebrew children were subject. Christ is the Man who endured affliction for His brethren, and delivered them with an outstretched arm. Christ is the Lamb slain to redeem a people from death. "*Christ our passover is sacrificed for us*" (1 Corinthians 5:7).

Take the second period: Egypt to Sinai (chapters 13–18).

The leader who guided the people through baptism into death by the power of resurrection surely points to Christ—the bread from heaven, the rock from which the waters gushed, and the captain who drives back the Amalekites, a type of the flesh. All these prefigured the Christ.

Take the third period: At Sinai (chapters 19–40).

We learn that we are under law to Christ. We have a Mediator in Christ. We have a High Priest in Christ. His torn flesh was the rent veil which gives the believer access into the holiest of all. If we are Christ's, we too are pilgrims journeying through a land of drought. The history of Israel in Exodus, while it stirs within us great searching of heart, at the same time suggests sweet consolation in Christ. "*O give thanks unto the Lord,...* [who] *brought out Israel from among them...with a strong hand, and a stretched out arm; for his mercy endureth for ever*" (Psalm 136:1, 11–12).

4. The Sinner

The story of Exodus is repeated in every soul that seeks deliverance from the enmeshing and enervating influences of the world. With this in view the book is human from the first verse to the last. The things that happened were by way of figure or example, and were written for our admonition. (See 1 Corinthians 10:11.)

1. Man forgets his origin as one made in the image of God and his destiny as one meant to live in the fear and favor of God. Alas, he turns from the source of blessing and is content to serve the devil. Pharaoh had no right to Israel's services. Israel belonged to God, but she forgot her divine call and the divine promises.
2. God's first work is to awaken the sinner to the shame and misery of his position. To this end the path of sin is made bitter. Languishing under an intolerable burden, the sinner sighs by reason of his bondage. Thus was it with Israel when conscience awoke under oppression.
3. After an awakening there follows a time of struggle. The soul tries to free itself. By reformation or religious efforts of the flesh, the sinner strives to plague the Pharaoh within him and escape from his hand. But all the plagues of Egypt were of little avail. Struggles were futile. Israel was thrust back upon God. So the sinner discovers that he cannot save himself.
4. At last the place of the shedding of blood is reached. At the foot of the cross, the burden rolls away. By the death and resurrection of his Substitute, the sinner escapes as a bird out of the snare of the fowler. The blood being sprinkled, the old master is defeated. Israel owed everything to the slain lamb. And Moses takes great care to impress upon the minds of his readers that deliverance from beginning to end is all of God.

5. Then comes separation. The old life is forsaken. Through death and resurrection there comes a new life. Out of Egypt, through the Red Sea, not a hoof is left behind. Then comes a life of dependence and obedience.
6. The next stage is guidance and instruction by the Spirit. Instruction is ever the necessary sequence of obedience. Life is lived within the holiest, and reflects the holiness and glory of the inner shrine. The soul is His peculiar possession.

ITS ANALYSIS

The following outline of Exodus is helpful:

1. *The Bondage* (chapters 1–6)

The changed conditions. Rapid increase of the people and their great oppression as a punishment for idolatry, which produced hatred of Egypt. The birth, training, and call of Moses. The new name (3:13–22). The divine "I wills" (6:3–8).

2. *Redemption* (chapters 7–12)

The contest between Jehovah and the gods of Egypt. The ten plagues and the victory of Jehovah. The first stage in the emancipation of Israel.

3. *Guidance* (chapters 13–18)

God's care of the pilgrims in their progress to Sinai. A manifestation of deliverance. The pillar of cloud and fire. The Red Sea. Marah and Elim. The manna and the smitten rock. Elevation of Moses' hands and Joshua's victory. Jethro's wise counsel.

4. *Law* (chapters 19–24)

At Sinai. The sanctification of the people and the covenant of the Law. Its ratification by blood. The vision of God and communion with God.

5. *Grace* (chapters 25–40)

The tabernacle was set up. Its apartments, furniture, sacrifices, and priesthood. It is wonderful as the earthly residence of Jehovah and as the figure of the body of Christ; also a figure of the church of Christ on earth (2 Corinthians 6:16) and in heaven (Hebrews 8:1–2). It is because of this precious truth that the description is so full and minute.

The Plagues of Egypt

As many are not aware of the significance of the plagues it may be found helpful to consider briefly these divine visitations upon Egypt. Ten plagues in all befell the Egyptians. Ten is a number suggesting the perfection of divine order. The whole cycle is complete; nothing is wanting. In the ten plagues we have the perfection of God's judgments against the gods of Egypt. (See Exodus 12:12; Acts 7:43.) Egypt was a land polluted by idolatry, and the plagues were remarkably adapted as punishment for stupid idolatries, monstrous wickednesses, and wanton cruelties.

Plague One: The Waters Turned to Blood (7:14–25)

The priests of Egypt held blood in abhorrence, yet they cruelly sported with the blood of the captive Israelites, whose children they caused to be cast into the river. The Egyptians worshipped the river Nile as a god, partly because of its delicious waters, but chiefly because of the extraordinary fertility of the land by its annual overflow. They called it "the Ocean or Sacred Nile." Yet its sacred waters were turned to blood. An object of worship was turned into an object of abhorrence.

Plague Two: The Frogs (8:1–15)

Frogs were consecrated to the deity of "Osiris," the greatest of the Egyptian gods. The swelling of frogs was regarded by the priests as an emblem of divine inspiration. This gross superstition was severely rebuked when swarms of these creatures filled the river and the land. Houses, beds, vessels of food, containing these objects of veneration, quickly made the whole country offensive.

Plague Three: The Lice (8:16–19)

The idolatries of Egypt were accompanied by the most unclean, foul, and abominable rites imaginable. Scrupulous external cleanliness, however, was observed by the priests. As no priest dared officiate with lice upon his garments, extreme cautiousness was constantly observed. Cleanliness was worshipped. This is why the plague of lice shocked and disgraced the priests and led the magicians to see in it the finger of God.

Plague Four: The Flies (8:20–32)

The Egyptians worshipped several deities whose province it was to drive away the flies which swarmed over the country during the summer season. The god of Ekrom, mentioned in 2 Kings 1:2, was a fly deity, and was known as Zebub or Beel-zebub, prince, lord, or god of flies. Strange, is it not, that this is the name given by our Lord to Satan? (See Matthew 12:24–27.)

Plague Five: The Pestilence of the Cattle (9:1–7)

Egypt also held many beasts in idolatrous veneration. The most outstanding beast deity was the sacred bull, Apis. The soul of their god Osiris was believed to reside in the body of this bull. Yet neither Osiris nor Apis could save the beasts of Egypt. The smiting of all the cattle was all the more grievous when it was realized that no injury had befallen the cattle of Israel.

Plague Six: The Boils (9:8–12)

Several medical deities, to whom on particular occasions living men were sacrificed, likewise held sway in the realm of worship. We read of Moloch (Acts 7:43), which was one of these gods. Those sacrificed to such a god were burnt alive upon the high altar, their ashes being cast into the air, so that with every scattered atom a blessing might descend. It has been suggested that Moses took ashes from the altar, ashes of human bodies offered to a medical deity, and cast them into the air; but the dust descended upon the priests and people, afflicting them with tormenting boils. By this plague all honored deities were shamed.

Plague Seven: Hail, Rain, Fire (9:13–35)

Isis and Osiris were the gods of water and fire and were worshipped as protectors. At the season when this seventh plague came, it never hailed or rained. With the destruction of barley, the supply of food was diminished. By the loss of flax, Egypt's extensive trade in fine linens was greatly spoiled. The gods of the weather were powerless to resist this devastating plague. Yet such a judgment was mixed with grace. (See chapter 9:32.)

Plague Eight: The Locusts (10:1–20)

Isis and Serapis were supposed to protect the country from locusts. West winds might bring these enemies, but an east wind the Egyptians never feared, seeing they had the protection of the Red Sea. But Egypt's gods failed, for the very east wind they revered became their destruction.

Plague Nine: The Darkness (10:21–29)

Egypt also worshipped Ra—the Sun God. Their monarch was called Pharaoh, Child of the Sun. (See references in Amos 5:26 and Acts 7:43 to heavenly objects of adoration.) Yet such gods were shown to be under control, for darkness plagued the earth, except in the dwellings of Israel where light prevailed.

Plague Ten: The Death of the Firstborn (11:12–36)

This last, terrible plague was directed against all the heathen deities at one time. *"Now I know that the Lord is greater than all gods: for in the thing wherein they dealt proudly he was above them"* (Exodus 18:11).

The principal reason of this final and heaviest calamity was to avenge their unlamented cruelties upon Israel. As God's firstborn, Egypt had oppressed her; now all the firstborn of Egypt are destroyed. Pharaoh wielded the absolute power of death, but judgment overtakes this autocrat, for *"from the firstborn of Pharaoh that sitteth upon his throne, even unto the firstborn of the maidservant that is behind the mill; and all the firstborn of beasts"* suffered in this righteous retribution (11:5). And this last judgment humbled the proud spirit of Pharaoh, causing him to release hastily the people of God.

The first two plagues were foretold by Moses and were imitated by the magicians. The rest they failed to copy and confessed that they were wrought by the finger or power of God.

The idol-worship of Egypt had its influence on Israel. (See Exodus 32:23; Acts 7:42.) Egypt had her sacred bull, Israel had her molten calf. In this generation we have great need to obey the injunction of the aged apostle John: *"Little children, keep yourselves from idols"* (1 John 5:21).

QUESTIONS FOR REVIEW

1. Explain the significance of the two titles of the book.
2. What are the New Testament references to the title?
3. Who wrote the book, and what qualifications had he?
4. How many years are covered by the book?
5. State the usage and significance of the word, "Passover."
6. Outline the purpose of Exodus, and name some of its leading ideas.
7. Indicate its connection with other books.
8. Explain the types found in Exodus.
9. How would you outline the book?
10. Describe the meaning of the plagues. Why were there ten?
11. In what way did Israel become idolatrous?

4

LEVITICUS: THE BOOK OF HOLINESS

INTRODUCTION

Doubtless, some have found the Book of Leviticus a weariness to the flesh. Its intimate descriptions of the sacrifices may seem pointless. Yet no book in the Bible is so wonderfully profitable, seeing that its study tends to deepen our adoration of Christ, whose face Leviticus so faithfully portrays. To the Jewish fathers the ceremonies of this third Pentateuchal book were signposts in the way of life, and if we read the book in the right way, we shall find in it the unsearchable riches of Christ.

ITS TITLE

Leviticus itself is taken from the Septuagint and means "The Levitical Book," seeing that it deals with the rites and ceremonies appointed in connection with the Levitical priesthood. It was the guidebook of the priests. (See Exodus 4:14; Hebrews 7:11.)

The Jews called it *Vayyikon,* being the Hebrew equivalent of the first three words of chapter 1, *"And he called."* The book contains God's call to worship and fellowship, to holiness of heart and habit.

The Babylonian Talmud, and also the Arabic and Syrian versions, refer to it as "The Law of the Priests," or "The Law of the Offerings," seeing that it treats of the sacrifices and services in charge of the Levitical priesthood.

The first and last titles are man-given. The second is the divine name and is more in keeping with the contents of the book. Levites are only twice mentioned in the book. (See 25:32–33).

Leviticus naturally follows Exodus. The tabernacle having been set up, its services and duties of the priests are now defined.

ITS AUTHOR

The first verse is explicit concerning this matter. *"The LORD called unto Moses."* Moses wrote by revelation of God. While this phrase refers particularly to the section which follows, the same or similar words are repeated some thirty-six times in the twenty-seven chapters. Thus the book is composed very largely of the actual words of Jehovah. (See Numbers 33:1–2; 2 Chronicles 30:16; Jeremiah 7:22–23; Ezekiel 20:11; Matthew 8:4; Romans 10:5; Galatians 3:12; 1 Peter 1:16.) The mercy seat was the place of appointed meeting and gracious revelation. (See Exodus 25:22; Numbers 7:8–9.)

ITS SCOPE

It covers the history of the first month of the second year after the departure of Israel from Egypt. The whole of the introduction given and the events recorded in this book come between April first, when the tabernacle was set up (see Exodus 40:2–17; Numbers 1:1), and May twentieth, when Israel departed from Mount Sinai (see Numbers 10:11). "Considered as embracing the history of one month only, this may claim to be the most remarkable book in the Old Testament."[10]

ITS KEYNOTE

Fellowship of a holy people with a holy God in worship and work. The dual thought of the book is:

1. How to obtain and make sure of this fellowship (1–16).
2. How to enjoy and improve such fellowship (17–27).

ITS KEY VERSE

Leviticus 19:2 has this distinction, "*Ye shall be holy.*" Thus the book is "The Textbook on Holiness." All who approach God, the priests who minister and the people who worship, must be holy. The redeemed must be holy because the Redeemer is holy. Priests, people, tabernacle, vessels, offerings, and garments had to be holy; that is, separate not only from sin but from common usage. "Holiness and its cognates occur some 131 times in the book. And such holiness is made possible by atonement." (See Leviticus 16:34; 17:11.)

---

10. Joseph Parker, *The People's Bible: Discourses upon Holy Scripture*, vol. 3 (London: Hazell, Watson, and Viney, 1885), 1.

ITS KEY WORD

To find out the characteristics of a book, one must note the words and phrases which frequently occur. That "holiness" is the characteristic feature of Leviticus is evident from the use of the word and its associates.

Holiness, sanctity, etc., occur 131 times; holiness itself 87 times.

Sacrifice, offering, and oblation, some 300 times.

Clean and unclean, 200 times.

Atonement, 45 times.

"*The* LORD *spake unto Moses,*" 36 times.

"*I am Jehovah,*" 21 times.

"*I am Jehovah your God,*" 21 times.

ITS PURPOSE

Primarily, the book teaches the great doctrines of purity, sanctification, separation, obedience, and service. It serves a manifold purpose:

1. It shows how God fulfilled His promise of Exodus 25:22.
2. It instructed Israel how to remain separate from the heathen.
3. It sought to train the people for the accomplishment of a worldwide mission.
4. It was a handbook for the priests to guide them in their work. It was the book of Israel's ritual. It is full

of principles for the guidance of the Aaronic priesthood and of those who desire to live in the enjoyment of priestly nearness to God.

5. It sets forth Christ and His full redemption by types and symbols. There is a starlight of Christ in all its ceremonies. Christ is in all, and all are in Him.

Forms may become obsolete, substance abides. Without Him the Pentateuch would have been impossible. He is the text of all the Old Testament. Because Old Testament history contains New Testament teaching, and because of the fulfillment of all the types in Christ, Leviticus is a manual of Christian theology, ethics, worship, and evidences.

ITS RELATION TO THE PENTATEUCH

Leviticus is linked to Exodus as Exodus is linked to Genesis. It is the central book in the heart of the Pentateuch. Sacrifice, its great theme, is the heart of salvation. Atonement is its central doctrine. It contains the third phase of redemption.

Genesis: The sin and ruin of man.

Exodus: The redemption and salvation of man.

Leviticus: The worship and communion of redeemed man.

Note the order observed here:

1. The origin of the plan of redemption and of the elect nation—Genesis.
2. The giving of that plan of redemption to the chosen people—Exodus.

3. The realization of redemption through God's presence in grace with the people—Leviticus.

Thus it is with ourselves. We came to God as lost sinners, and appropriating by faith a blood-bought salvation we were brought nigh. Sacrifice is now the basis of true worship. The Lord Jesus Christ is our great High Priest in the presence of God for us. And the Christian's only place of worship is inside the veil.

Leviticus, then, is "the Gospel of the Pentateuch, glistening with purity, turning law into music, and spreading a banquet in the wilderness."[11] Holiness, without which no man shall see the Lord, pervades the whole book and all the varied ceremonial. God is holy and man is sinful and under sentence of death. God in grace draws near to man, and appoints the way of sacrifice as a propitiation for sin. In mercy He accepts the death of the sacrifice for the death of the sinner. Atonement is through the blood shed and the blood sprinkled. All looks forward to Christ, by and in whose blood there is propitiation and atonement. What a gospel to preach, even from Leviticus!

ITS PECULIARITIES

There are several unique features that one can gather up and use with much profit in teaching Leviticus:

1. The truth written large over the book is that God must be approached in the way of His appointing, and that by sacrifice. (See Leviticus 8:36; 9:6–7.)
2. It insists upon holiness of body as well as of soul. God's people must be holy all through, in things both great

11. Parker, *The People's Bible*, 9.

and small. (See Leviticus 19:2; 1 Corinthians 10:31; Colossians 3:17; 1 Peter 3:10–11.)

3. Holiness must characterize our very eating. The dietary of Moses has been highly approved by men of science.
4. The Holy Spirit is not once named, although referred to in all the other books of the Pentateuch. Nevertheless He is in the background, seeing that it is His work to glorify Christ. (See John 16:14.)
5. Its most conspicuous chapter is the sixteenth—the great day of atonement. The slain goat represents guilt expiated by blood, and the scapegoat declares the removal of the offense from before the face of God. (Scapegoat—*Azazel*—means removal.) There is grace in its two aspects, namely, the passing over of transgression and the remembering of it no more. (See Micah 7:18–19; Hebrews 8:12; and other atonement chapters—Genesis 22; Exodus 12; Numbers 14).
6. The central person is Aaron, the high priest, who is a fitting type of Christ, our great High Priest.
7. Various words are used for "offerings":

   (1) *Qorban*: something brought near to God at the altar, for acceptance as a gift or for judgment as a sacrifice. (See Leviticus 1 and 2.)

   (2) *Minchah*: a present, freely made, to show one's love or to get and keep someone's favor. (See Genesis 4 and 5.)

(3) *Terumah*—a part, contribution or share, as part of the dough, the harvest, or the meat offering. (Leviticus 22:12.)

The offerings were of two kinds:

(1) Sweet savor. Pleasing to and accepted by God, as the burnt, meal, or peace offerings.

(2) Non-sweet savor. Seeing that they were so closely identified with sin, such as the sin and trespass offerings.

ITS PRESENT VALUE

Leviticus is an indispensable book and should be studied along with Hebrews, its New Testament counterpart. It is a key to the New Testament teaching on the atonement. It is a book of illustrations on the way of salvation. The Epistle to the Hebrews is an inspired commentary upon the Book of Leviticus, from which we learn that the Hebrew ritual was the gospel of Christ, exhibited in symbols and shadows to the Israelites. Carrying, then, a symbolic setting-forth of the gospel, and being so full of Christ and of the gospel of the grace of God, Leviticus is of supreme value to the student of the Bible.

The book is full of the truth that saves and sanctifies. The cross has solved the enigmatic laws and closed the temple. Under it the ephod ceases and the unction of the king passes away. The law prepares for the introduction of Christianity and for the understanding of the person, mission, and work of Christ. It was a pedagogue for the guidance and control of Israel until Christ came.

ITS ANALYSIS

That there are various ways of outlining the contents of Leviticus is evident from a comparison of outlines as given by gifted Bible students. Here, for example, is a very simple yet efficient analysis:

1. Sacrifice (chapters 1–7). Worship must be based on sacrifice appointed by God and acceptable to God.
2. Priesthood (chapters 8–10). Worship must be through a Mediator. No man cometh unto the Father but by the Son. (See John 14:6.)
3. Purification (chapters 11–16). Worship must be with clean hands and a pure heart. Without holiness no man shall see the Lord.
4. Festivals (chapters 17–21). Worship must be social and gladsome, at stated times and in fixed places.
5. Idolatry (chapters 22–26). Worship must be with the whole heart.
6. Vows (chapter 27). Worship must be with the making and keeping of vows, but only such as ought to be made.

Further, Leviticus is a book of laws as distinguished from "the book of the Law." The latter term includes the whole of the Pentateuch, but the laws in Leviticus are a development and amplification of the Law given at Sinai. With this thought in mind, one well-known expositor has given us the following unique outline.

Access (chapters 1–16)	*Holiness* (17–27)
The Way to God by Sacrifice	The Walk with God by Sanctification
1. The Law of Offerings (1–7): Burnt (1); Meat (2); Peace (3); Sin (4); Trespass (5–6:7); Law of Offerings (6:8–7:38).	1. The Law of Holiness (17–22): Personal (17); Sacrifice, Warnings, Directions, Family (18); Obedience, Unlawful Marriages, Warnings, Social (19–20); Priestly, Holiness, Marriage, Bodily Perfection and Purity (21–22).
2. The Law of the Priesthood (8–10): A. Appointments (8): Called (8:1–5); Cleansed (8:6); Clothed (8:7–13); Consecrated (8:14–36). B. Qualifications (9): Sympathy (9:1–8); Sacrifice (9:9–21); Intercession (9:22–24). C. Failure (10): Nadab and Abihu.	2. The Law of Feasts (23): Passover (23:4–5); Unleavened Bread (23:6–8); Firstfruits (23:9–14); Wave-loaves (23:15–22); Trumpets (23:22–25); Day of Atonement (23:26–38); tabernacles (23:39–44). (Consecration and punishment, chapter 24.)
3. The Law of Purity (11–16): Pure Food (11); Pure Bodies (12–13:46); Pure Garments (13:47–14:32); Pure Homes (14:33–57); Provision for Impurity—Atonement (16).	3. The Law of the Land (25–27): Sabbatic Year (25:1–7); Jubilee (25:8–55); Obedience and Disobedience (26); Vows and Tithes (27).

The student is referred to a similar but fuller outline in Dr. G. Campbell Morgan's "Analyzed Bible" series.[12]

Before concluding the study of this most fascinating book it will be profitable to devote some little space to the typical value of the offerings and the priesthood. The multiplicity of rites, with which the book is filled, form a proof of the insufficiency of the Levitical system to take away sin. Christ's death and resurrection, however, make all of these rites so luminous.

THE TYPES IN LEVITICUS

What a variety of sacrifices there were which God provided in old time for the people of His possession! Continually the altars flamed and smoked. Continually the knife was raised, and the animals were slain. Continually the priests must mediate between the people and the thrice-holy Lord.

The Sweet Offerings

That is, those that were pleasing to and accepted by God.

The Burnt Offering

This offering daily pointed to Jesus, who for us and our salvation so willingly offered Himself to God as a sacrifice without spot or blemish. And this offering speaks of His entire dedication and is typical of the One who was wholly surrendered to God and His service even unto death. An unflinching devotion is the burnt offering He expects from each one of us.

12. G. Campbell Morgan, *The Analyzed Bible*, vol. 1 (New York: Fleming H. Revell Company, 1907), 52.

The Meat or Meal Offering

This only bloodless offering demanded by God betokens the pure humanity that Christ was able to lay on the altar of sacrifice in obedience to God's perfect will. His human perfection, tested by suffering, satisfied the heart of God, when His Son tabernacled thirty-three years in human flesh. And is this not an example to us that our daily labor, energy, and toil should be devoted to His praise?

The Peace Offering

Christ is here seen making peace by the blood of His cross. Friendship and fellowship are ours as the result of His perfect sacrifice. Christ crucified is the basis of all friendly intercourse between God and man. What a blessed offering this is, an emblem of the feast of salvation and friendship at which He sits down to eat and drink with men!

The Non-Sweet Offerings

That is, those which were so definitely associated with sin.

The Sin Offering

The sin offering carries the humbling message of the impossibility of man's nullifying the guilt of the soul, and of the absolute need of expiation. The sinner's guilt and its removal by the sacrifice of a substituted victim is the gospel of this offering. Christ as our propitiation is hereby seen. Willingly He shed His blood for us, and suffered outside the gate.

The Trespass Offering

Man's trespasses or sins are debts, that is, definite acts of wrong or evil. In killing the offering, the sinner was regarded as rendering satisfaction and reparation through his substitute. This offering was designed to convict the children of Israel of their fraudulence in depriving God and men of their dues and to portray the penitence which heaven requires—a penitence which is restitution as well as confession. From this offering we learn that Christ discharges our debt, repairs our wrongs, and redeems our life to God. If the debt was against the Lord, sacrifice preceded reparation; if against man, reparation preceded sacrifice. (See Matthew 5:23–24.) An Israelite with a guilty conscience and a remembrance of sin had practically to begin at the end of the series. Such is the divine order of thought. The human order, however, is exactly the reverse. Beginning with the guilt-offering, one ends with the burnt-offering. From the remission of sins we advance to offer ourselves in entire dedication.

Dr. Alexander Smellie's comment on "a sacrifice of richer blood" is most fitting at this point.

> There is but one sacrifice, all-sufficing, acceptable, wanting in nothing—the sacrifice of Christ, both Victor and Victim.
>
> Did He not make Himself a burnt offering, yielding His life to His Father, that in perfect submission and glad obedience He might keep the commandment which I had broken and cast aside?
>
> Was He not by His own choice and will the true meal offering, tasking Himself morning, noon and night in the service of God, and esteeming the task not a bondage but a boon?

Is He not my peace offering, without blemish, without compare?—for through Him I have the good will and tender love of the far- and heart-searching Lord. I sit down under His shadow with great delight and His fruit is sweet to my taste.

Sin offering He is, too; He who is at once the blameless Lamb and the merciful and faithful High Priest, shedding His life-blood on the sacrificial tree to atone for my evil. One drop of it effaces the blackest record. For the sake of one ruddy drop my condemnation is cancelled, and I have an unalterable pardon and an abiding rest.

And, beyond doubt, Jesus Christ is the trespass offering for my derelict soul, paying to the last farthing the awful debt which I could never pay, and bringing me out of the bankrupt's prison to citizenship and freedom, use and fame. In the end of the age God provides for me a many-colored salvation, and a Saviour whose infinitude of worth can never be told.

On His dear head my faith would lay her trembling and appropriating hand, simply to His Cross I cling—to His Cross and to Himself. He is all my boast, and, as Wesley's hymn phrases it, "I enjoy His glorious infamy!"[13]

The Typical Teaching of Priesthood

Aaron and his sons were called to function as priests, and can be made to typify Christ and believers. We have been made

13. Alexander Smellie, *In the Secret Place: A Book of Daily Devotional Meditations* (London: Andrew Melrose, 1907), 64.

unto Him a kingdom of priests. Aspects like the following can be developed:

1. They were divinely chosen and called.

So the divine purpose of His choice of us is that we might be holy and without blame before Him in love. (See Ephesians 1:4.)

2. They had to be washed with water.

God cannot use a defiled saint. Washing is therefore necessary. (See 1 John 1:7, 9.) Our laver of cleansing from the defilement of sin is the Word. (See Ephesians 5:26.)

3. They had to be rightly clothed.

Thus is it with the saint, whose whole armor is provided for him in Ephesians 6:10–19.

4. They had to be anointed with oil.

Surely this answers to the saint's endowment of the Holy Spirit for sanctification and service. (See 1 John 2:27; Acts 1:8.)

5. They had to be consecrated.

We dedicate; God consecrates. Ear, thumb, and toe had to be marked. Witness, work, and walk are under divine control. All we dedicate is in virtue of Christ's sacrifice. (See Romans 12:1–2.)

In the destruction of Nadab and Abihu we are warned against the sin of presumption and self-will. Approaching God after the desires of our heart, or neglecting or despising the ordinances of a divinely-prescribed sacrifice, is the offering of a strange fire. Departing from the cross in precept or practice, our priestly influence is stained.

The Typical Teaching of the Law of Purity

For a thorough study of the typical import, not only of Leviticus but all of the Pentateuch, one is recommended to that excellent series known as *C. H. M.'s Notes.*[14] These books are worth their weight in gold.

1. Leprosy

Once in the blood, this dread disease became overt in loathsome ways. Body, clothes, and home were alike affected. And, moreover, it was incurable insofar as human means were concerned.

The leper could not help himself. (See Romans 4:4–5.)

The priest sought the leper, not the leper the priest. (See Luke 19:10.)

The shedding of blood was necessary before healing could be granted. (See Hebrews 9:22.)

In the two birds (Leviticus 14:5–7), a glorious truth is unfolded. One was slain in an earthen vessel over running water. (See Romans 4:25, 8:2; 1 Peter 3:18.) The other was dipped in the blood of its fellow and released. (See Romans 4:25; 1 Corinthians 15:17.) Faith is vain if Christ was not raised again, for we are still moral lepers.

2. Food

In this divine picture-book we discover a God who hates sin and who makes every provision for the holiness of His own.

---

14. Lockyer is referring to a six-volume set by Charles H. Mackintosh, published by the Fleming H. Revell Company, often called *Notes on the Pentateuch* or simply *Notes.* The volume on Leviticus was likely first published in 1860. —*Editor's Note*

The Beasts

Two things were essential to render them clean. They had to chew the cud and divide the hoof. These two had to go together. Failing to conform to this dual necessity, the beast was immediately rejected. Why? Well, for these reasons: the chewing of the cud is a natural process and indicates the inward digestion of what is eaten. Superficial reading of the Scriptures is not enough. It is necessary to eat the Word of God as food for our souls. (See Jeremiah 15:16.) The divided hoof sets forth the character of one's natural walk. A mere outward life is not sufficient. The inner life and outer walk must be in complete harmony.

The Fish

The people could only eat the fish which had fins and scales. Again, a double work: a fish with a "fin" which would enable it to move along in the water; "scales" to resist the action of the water—a double provision. So the believer needs "fins" or spiritual power to move onward and upward through life; "scales" or spiritual protection to resist the influence of the world. The Spirit alone can enable us to resist such a penetrating influence. Getting on with some Christians means getting in, that is, into the world. To get on spiritually, therefore, we must get out of many things.

The Birds

The Israelite had to live on those birds that did not feed on flesh. Birds eating carrion were counted unclean, just as creeping things were reckoned unclean. And the believer can only thrive on the right kind of spiritual food. There is no sustenance in anything carnal. The Christian must not creep on or cling to the earth but use his wings.

Perhaps nothing has ever been written in so small a compass that so accurately expresses the typical and evangelical nature of the historical ordinances of the Christian faith, as the following verses of the poet Cowper:

> Israel in ancient days
> Not only had a view
> Of Sinai in a blaze,
> But learned the Gospel too.
> The types and figures were a glass
> In which they saw the Saviour's face.
>
> The Paschal sacrifice
> And blood-besprinkled door,
> Seen with enlightened eyes
> And once applied with power,
> Would end the need of other blood
> To reconcile the world to God.
>
> The lamb, the door set forth
> His perfect innocence,
> Whose blood of matchless worth
> Should be the soul's defense;
> For He who can for sin atone
> Must have no failings of His own.
>
> The scapegoat on his head
> The People's trespass bore,
> And to the desert led

Was to be seen no more;
In Him one surely seemed to say
Behold, I bear your sins away.

Dipt in his fellow's blood
The living bird went free,
The type well understood
Explained the sinner's plea;
Described a guilty soul enlarged
And by a Saviour's death discharged.

Jesus, I love to trace
Throughout the sacred page
The footsteps of Thy grace,
The same in every age.
O grant that I may faithful be
To clearer light vouchsafed to me.[15]

Inspiration can also be gained from a prayerful reading of Isaac Watts' poem:

Not all the blood of beasts
On Jewish altars slain,
Could give the guilty conscience peace,
Or wash away the stain.

But Christ, the heav'nly Lamb,
Takes all our sins away—
A sacrifice of nobler name,
And richer blood than they.

---

15. William Cowper, "The Old-Testament Gospel," *Olney Hymns* (1779).

My faith would lay her hand
On that dear head of Thine,
While like a penitent I stand,
And there confess my sin.

Believing, we rejoice
To see the curse remove;
We bless the Lamb with cheerful voice,
And sing His bleeding love.[16]

Occasionally we meet with those who find themselves at a loss for sermonic material. Picking away at an isolated text or two the barrel quickly empties. And yet, with such an inexhaustible store as is found in Leviticus, one should never find it difficult to secure a theme. Contemporary culture may rebel at typical preaching, yet there is no phase of Bible presentation which can keep a preacher so fresh and interesting. If these lines are being read by someone who finds sermonic preparation hard, let him take up a course of addresses on the tabernacle and its offerings, and he will find his own love for Christ strengthened and an ever-larger company of people to listen to his ministrations. To aid the preacher, I'm including the below tabular treatment that can be used with great effect.

16. Isaac Watts, "Not All the Blood of Beasts," 1709.

The Levitical Offerings

(Read Hebrews with Leviticus)

No.	Offering	Scripture Reference	Typical Teaching	Law of Offering	N.T. Parallel
1.	Burnt Offering	Leviticus 1:1–17	Christ offering Himself without spot to God	Leviticus 6:8–13	2 Corinthians 5:21; Ephesians 5:2; 1 Peter 1:19–21
2.	Meat Offering	Leviticus 2:1–16	Christ in His human perfection tested by suffering	Leviticus 6:14–23	Hebrews 5:8–9; 6:15
3.	Peace Offering	Leviticus 3:1–17	Christ our Peace	Leviticus 7:11–21	Ephesians 2:14–18; Colossians 1:20–22
4.	Sin Offering	Leviticus 4:1–35	Christ atoning for guilt of sin	Leviticus 6:24–30	Hebrews 10:19–22; 13:11, 12
5.	Trespass Offering	Leviticus 5:1–19	Christ atoning for pollution of sin	Leviticus 7:1–7	Titus 2:14; 1 John 1:7–9

The Feasts of Jehovah

No.	Feast	Scripture Reference	Typical Teaching	O.T. Reference	N.T. Parallel
1.	Passover	Leviticus 23:4, 5	Christ our Redeemer	Leviticus 16	1 Corinthians 5:7
2.	Unleavened Bread	Leviticus 23:6–8	Communion of saints with Christ	Deuteronomy 16:3	1 Corinthians 5:6–8; 1 Corinthians 10:16
3.	Firstfruits	Leviticus 23:9–14	Christ's Resurrection	Exodus 23:19	1 Corinthians 15:20–23
4.	Wave Loaves or Weeks	Leviticus 23:15–22	Descent of the Holy Spirit	Deuteronomy 16:10	Acts 2:1–4; 1 Corinthians 12:3–11
5.	Trumpets	Leviticus 23:23–25	Israel's awakening and repentance	Isaiah 27:12, 13; Joel 2:15–32	Matthew 24:29–31; 1 Thessalonians 4:16
6.	Day of Atonement	Leviticus 23:26–32	Israel's cleansing and restoration	Leviticus 16:30; Zechariah 13:1	Hebrews 9:1–28
7.	Tabernacles	Leviticus 23:33–44	Israel in the land, the Millennium	Ezra 3:4; Zechariah 14:16–19	Ephesians 2:19–22; Revelation 21:3–5

QUESTIONS FOR REVIEW

1. Do you think a study of Leviticus is profitable? Why?
2. How does the Jewish title of Leviticus describe its contents?
3. Could you prove that Moses wrote the book? How?
4. Set forth the chronology of Leviticus.
5. Indicate the distinctive key verse.
6. State some characteristic key words.
7. What would you say is the dual thought of Leviticus?
8. Suggest some of the primary purposes of the book.
9. Trace its connections with the rest of the Pentateuch.
10. Outline some of its peculiar features.
11. Has Leviticus any present-day value? If so, describe.
12. Give an outline of its contents.
13. Briefly state the typical significance of the offerings and the Aaronic priesthood.
14. How many feasts are mentioned in Leviticus? Name them.

5

NUMBERS: THE BOOK OF WANDERING

INTRODUCTION

When General William Booth was asked to record something in a princess's autograph album, he wrote, "Saved to Serve." And so Israel, too, was "saved to serve." All service requires prayer, faith and effort; but effort to be faithful must be methodical. "Order is heaven's first law,"[17] and in Numbers we see God, as a God of order, organizing the people for entering into and taking possession of the land.

ITS TITLE

In the Septuagint or Greek Old Testament, we find that the word *Arithmi,* which was rendered "Numeri" in the Vulgate,

17. Alexander Pope, "An Essay on Man" (1734), Epistle IV, line 49.

has passed into the Authorized Version as "Numbers." It was so called because of the two numberings of the nation—one before leaving Sinai, the other before entering Canaan.

In the Hebrew Bible the book is called *Bemidhar* or, "In the wilderness" (1:1), a title describing the real contents of Numbers.

ITS AUTHOR

Moses, the man of Jehovah, a wise counsellor, the ideal prophet, and a friend of God. (See Numbers 11:17.) "*Moses wrote their goings*" is sufficient proof of the Mosaic authorship of both Leviticus and Numbers. (See Numbers 33:1–2).

ITS SCOPE

About forty years are covered. (See Numbers 14:34; Deuteronomy 1:2–3.) Forty is the probation number; thus testing and trial are prominent in the book. When we come to Hebrews, it is to find that God forgets these wasted years. Hebrews 11:29 finishes with the Red Sea, and the next verse (11:30) commences with the walls of Jericho falling down. Forty years of wandering forgotten! How like God! "*Their sins and iniquities will I remember no more*" (Hebrews 10:17).

ITS KEYNOTE

Briefly summarized, the leading messages are these:

1. The majesty, holiness, and presence of God. (Note recurrences of the divine "I.")
2. The land by right as a gift became Israel's in fact by conquest.

3. A holy God and a holy people in a holy land.
4. Organization in life and work. (Organized effort is our duty.)
5. Failure because of discontent and disobedience.
6. The necessity of watchfulness against unbelief and murmuring.
7. God's patience with, provision for, and protection of His redeemed people. (See Deuteronomy 8:4.)

ITS KEY VERSE

"*We are journeying unto the place of which the* L*ORD said, I will give it to you.... These are the journeys of the children of Israel*" (Numbers 10:29; 33:1).

ITS KEY WORDS

Work, war, wandering. The experience was an up-and-down one, but Canaan was ultimately reached.

ITS FORM

It is partly legislation and partly history, but of nearly the whole period of forty years there is scarcely any record. Sin spells silence. Numbers is a book of wanderings, warfare, work, and wickedness.

ITS RELATION TO THE PENTATEUCH

It is the fourth book in the Pentateuch and is vitally connected with Leviticus. The conjunction "and" of 1:1 gives us the literary connection of Numbers with Leviticus. A more definite relationship, however, is suggested. The covenant had been made and confirmed; the Law had been given. Now the people had to be prepared to mete out to the Canaanites a judgment overdue. Thus the tribes were organized in a military fashion in order that Jehovah, who dwelt in their midst, might lead them into the land which was theirs by right through the gift of God, but had to be theirs in fact by actual conquest.

Comparing the book with other Pentateuchal books, we have:

Genesis, Creation and Fall: Divine Choice.

Exodus, Redemption by Blood: Divine Deliverance.

Leviticus, Worship and Fellowship: Divine Holiness.

Numbers, Service and Walk: Divine Discipline.

Deuteronomy, Instruction and Direction: Divine Counsel.

The more one studies the books of the Bible, the more one is convinced that the mind of God was at work not only in their compilation but in their very arrangement.

ITS CHARACTERISTICS

Several features peculiar to this book are full of instruction. Some of these have been gleaned in our study:

Candor

The faults not only of the people but also of the leaders—Miriam, Aaron, and Moses—are fully exposed. This is a characteristic feature of the Bible as a whole. Angel heights and devil depths in human life are laid bare.

Fragments of Ancient Poetry

1. *The Priestly Blessing* (6:24–26). The Jews discovered the Trinity in these verses.
2. *The Signal Chants* (10:35–36). These chants which were sung when the signals were given for the moving of the Ark and the whole camp are precious odes.
3. *The Book of the Wars of Jehovah* (21:14–15). This volume was probably a collection of hymns celebrating the mighty acts of the Lord on behalf of His people.
4. *The Song of the Well* (21:16–25). Doubtless this song was inspired by the discovery of a well during the march.
5. *Proverbs of Victory* (21:27–30). These were used to celebrate the destruction of the chief cities of the Amorites.
6. *The Ribbon of Blue* (15:38). Every person had to wear this ribbon of blue upon their garments. Blue, the heavenly color, reminded the people that as servants of God they had to be heavenly in obedience and character and separate from earthly ambitions and desires. This attractive sign marked them out as the people of God, whose commandments they were bound to obey. The Pharisees enlarged upon this requirement as a sign of unusual sanctity. (See Matthew 23:5.) Perhaps it was this part of the Lord's garment that the woman touched. (See Luke 8:44.)

A Book of Murmurings

Israel was slow to learn that godliness with contentment is great gain. (See 1 Timothy 6:6.) In spite of the mercy of God, they murmured. Grace did not keep them from grumbling, as will be readily noted by the following:

1. *The People Murmured at Taberah (11:1–3)*

Taberah means "burning" and possibly was so named because it was at this place that fire burnt some of the Israelites. Here the people murmured against the *way* God had led them. They likewise murmured at the *food* He fed them (11:4–35). What base ingratitude it was for them to yearn for the fleshpots of Egypt!

2. *The People Murmured at Hazeroth (12)*

Hazeroth signifies a court or enclosure. This place witnessed a grievous complaint over the *leader* God had set over them. Poor Moses, like many another leader, was the butt of jealousy.

3. *The People Murmured at Paran (13–14:30)*

Paran, meaning "beauty, glory, or ornament," was a district of caverns beautified with coral reefs. There the Israelites murmured at the *land* God had promised them. They also murmured against the *righteous verdict* which God had pronounced (14:40–45). It was here that they also murmured against God's *appointment for the priesthood* (chapters 16 and 17). Chapter 16 gives us Korah's instruction and destruction. Chapter 17 records Aaron's supremacy.

4. *The People Murmured at Kadesh (20:1–13)*

Kadesh means "holy place" and is from the word "to sanctify." There they murmured because of their *thirst,* wishing that they had died in Egypt.

5. The People Murmured at Edom (21:4–9)

Edom means to be red or earthy. There they loathed the *provision of God* and were plagued with serpents for their discontent with heavenly food.

What a sad record! Yes, and what a solemn warning this book carries for our own hearts. Let us beware of the initial sin of discontent or grumbling. We often look upon grumbling as a little sin, and not until we try to check ourselves do we find how completely it possesses us, and how it is ready to spring upon us at all hours of the day under the slightest provocation. The weather is bad, the tea is too sweet, the chops are half cold, the potatoes are not cooked, the package we expected is not delivered, and we complain. It was a secret heart-grumble that led to Eve's disobedience.

Tracing Israel's downward course in Numbers, we discover that the people journeyed from discontent to lust, to rebellion, to idolatry. So to be saved from this evil is one step toward perfection. (See Philippians 2:14; 1 Thessalonians 5:18.) In trying circumstances, special temptations, weak nerves, and depressions of spirit, give thanks. Such a shout of faith and song of praise causes the enemy to flee and leads to victory.

THE TYPES IN NUMBERS

In this book, when the holiness of God demands the holiness of His people, and the perils of idolatry with its heathen orgies and abominable customs are laid bare, one can find many forceful types of Christ, and of what He requires from His own.

Types of Christ

The Bread of Life (Numbers 11:7–9; John 6: 57, 58)

The Water of Life (Numbers 20:11; John 7:37; 1 Corinthians 10:4)

The Serpent lifted up. (Numbers 21:9; John 3:14, 15)

The Star out of Jacob (Numbers 24:17; Luke 1:78; 2 Peter 1:19; Revelation 2:28; 22:16)

The Nazarite Vow (Numbers 6:1–21; Nazarite means *one separated*; Hebrews 7:26)

The Rod of Aaron (Numbers 17:1–13; Christ's resurrection declares that He is appointed of God as the great High Priest.)

The Red Heifer (Numbers 19:1–10; This is a peculiar type of Christ through whose blood the believer can be cleansed from sin; the water represents the Word and the Spirit; and the ashes which gave the cleansing efficacy represent the sacrifice of Christ.)

The Cities of Refuge (Numbers 35:1–34; these typify shelter from judgment; Romans 8:1, 33–34; Hebrews 6:18–20)

The life of Moses as leader, teacher, and intercessor speaks of Christ.

Types of Believers

The history of Israel sojourning in the wilderness is reenacted in the lives of many saints. Divinely called, delivered, and made holy, the people yet experienced arrested progress. There is hardly any record of those sad thirty-eight years but a list of places where the camp rested, most of which are now quite unknown. Israel was a nation marking time, waiting for death; and they teach us that a life of sin and disobedience is ever a wasted life.

The people had to come back to Kadesh. If a believer has lost his joy, his freshness, his power, because of arrested progress, there is only one cure. He must get back to the place where he disobeyed God, confess his sin, and renew the life of obedience. With such a renewal there is likewise the renewal of joy and power.

Some of the people were kept out of the land by ignorance as well as disobedience. They started well but were robbed of the full enjoyment of all that God had promised them. Truly, many saints are still in the wilderness. The radiant look has gone. Weary and tired, the way has become hard and difficult. Complacently, the wilderness is endured with the hope that death will bring them into the Promised Land. But the Promised Land is not heaven. There are no wars in heaven, such as Israel experienced in Canaan. For us the Promised Land is a life of peace, holiness, and joy which we can enter now. Certainly there are enemies, giants, and walled cities, but we are well able to overcome them. Our Leader is unconquerable, so let us arise and possess our possessions.

ITS PRESENT VALUE

1. A record of the life and fortunes of the Hebrew nation under Moses before they settled in Canaan.
2. Israel is Jehovah's son, and as such is the object of perpetual care and discipline.
3. There is need for the priestly view of salvation with its emphasis on holiness, and for the prophetic view of salvation with its emphasis on righteousness.
4. Happiness and holiness are helps to health.

ITS ANALYSIS

The contents of this Book of Wandering have been classified in the following interesting way:

1. *At Sinai* (1:1 to 10:10): Number and Order. A period of nineteen days in preparation for departure from Sinai on the twentieth day of the second month of the second year after the Exodus.

A. Numbering and ordering the people (chapters 1–4)

B. Cleansing and blessing (chapters 5, 6)

C. Offerings of princes and dedication of altar (chapters 7, 8)

D. Passover, cloud, and trumpets (chapter 9:1–10:10)

2. *From Sinai to Kadesh* (10:11 to 14:45): Faithlessness and Failure. A period of eleven days, from the twentieth to the thirtieth of the second month in the second year after their departure from Egypt.

A. First march with the tabernacle (10:11–36)

B. Murmuring of the people (11:1–22)

C. Spirit given to elders (11:23–35)

D. Sedition of Miriam and Aaron (12)

E. Mission of the spies (chapters 13, 14)

3. *Wanderings in the Desert* (chapters 15 to 19): Trial and Discipline. A period of thirty-seven years, from the end of the second year to the beginning of the fortieth year. A sad section.

A. Laws for life in the land (chapter 15)

B. Rebellion of Korah (chapter 16)

C. Budding of Aaron's rod (chapter 17)

D. Position and work of Levites (chapter 18)

E. Cleansing from defilement (chapter 19)

4. *From Kadesh to Moab* (chapters 20 to 36): Judgment and Mercy. A period of ten months, from the beginning of the fortieth year.

A. Events on the journey (chapters 20, 21)

B. Balaam and Israel (chapters 22–25)

C. Second census and new leader (chapters 26, 27)

D. Sacrifices and vows (chapters 28–30)

E. War with Midian (chapter 31)

F. Partition of the land (chapters 32–34)

G. Cities of Refuge (chapter 35)

H. Marriage of heiresses (chapter 36).

Outline of Numbers in Three Parts

The analysis by Dr. G. Campbell Morgan is also very helpful. Years ago I purchased the outlines of the books of the Bible by this gifted expositor and pasted them in my teacher's Bible. And what a help they have been!

From Sinai to Kadesh was a journey of eleven days. (See Deuteronomy 1:2.) Because of unbelief and disobedience it was prolonged to forty years. The Israelites were made to sojourn in the wilderness a year for every day that the spies were in the land. (See Numbers 14:34.)

The wilderness was a part of the necessary discipline of a redeemed people, but not the long years of wandering. The latter were due to the unbelief of the people at Kadesh-barnea.

ANALYSIS OF NUMBERS

<table>
<tr><td>At Sinai
(1–10:10)</td><td>In the Wilderness
(10:11–19)</td><td>On the Border
(20–36)</td></tr>
<tr><td>The Order of the Camp (1–4):
Service.
The Purity of the Camp (5–6):
Sanitation.
The Worship of the Camp (6–9:14):
Sanctity.
The Movement of the Camp (9:15–10:10):
Guidance.</td><td>Discontent (11–17):
Against God by His people (11:1–3);
Against Circumstances (11:4–32);
Against Moses (chapter 12);
Against the Promised Land (13–14:38);
Against God's Verdict (14:39–15);
Against Appointments (16–17).
Direction (18 and 19):
Heave Offering (18);
Red Heifer (19).</td><td>At Kadesh (20 and 21):
Thirst and Rock (20:1–13);
Aaron's Death (20:23–29);
Serpents (21).
At Moab (22–36):
Balaam and Israel (22–25);
Second Census (26);
Sacrifice and Vows (27–30);
War with Midian (31);
Partition of Land (32);
Summaries (33–36).</td></tr>
<tr><td colspan="3">Time Covered by the Whole 36 Chapters</td></tr>
<tr><td>20 Days (cf. 1:1 with 10:11)</td><td>38 years, 10 months</td><td>9 months, 10 days</td></tr>
<tr><td colspan="3">Lessons to Be Learned from These Periods</td></tr>
<tr><td>God's Sovereignty and Provision</td><td>Trial and Failure</td><td>Judgment and Mercy</td></tr>
</table>

A Map of the Wanderings

The accompanying map will help to visualize the checkered career of Israel.

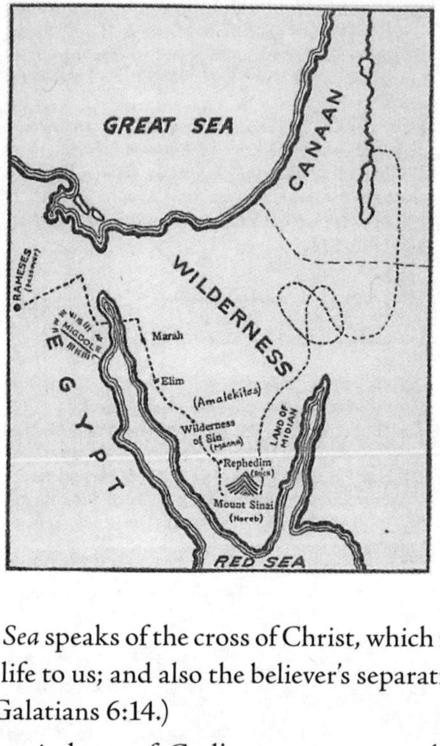

The *Red Sea* speaks of the cross of Christ, which meant death for Him but life to us; and also the believer's separation from the world. (See Galatians 6:14.)

Marah reminds us of God's power to turn the untoward experiences of life into blessings. (See Exodus 15:23.)

Elim is typical of the same power to give us rest and refreshment by the way. (See Exodus 15:27.) So far the path was and is of God.

Sinai testifies of God's holiness and of our own inherent evil—the experience of Romans 7:7–24.

But from *Kadesh-barnea* to *Jordan,* all that happened to Israel is for our warning, not imitation. (See 1 Corinthians 10:1–11; Hebrews 3:17–19.) Canaan rest can be ours here and now. (See Hebrews 4:4.)

The Tabernacle

Chapter 3 gives the resting order of the camp.

The following diagram will make the instructions covering Israel's camp life clear to the mind.

The tabernacle in the midst of the camp of Israel is a figure of Christ as the Center of all things.

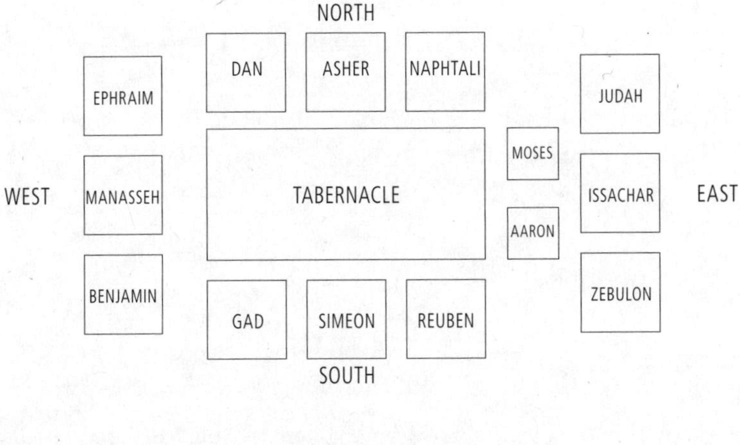

"Every man of the children of Israel shall pitch by his own standard, with the ensign of their father's house" (Numbers 2:2).

The Camps	The Ensign	The Tribes	Their Numbers	Their Position
Judah (2:3)	A Lion (Gen. 49:9; Ezek. 1:10; Rev. 4:7; 5:5).	Judah Issachar Zebulun	74,600 54,400 57,400	East
Reuben (2:10)	A Man (Gen. 30:14; Ezek. 1:10; Rev. 4:7).	Reuben Simeon Gad	46,500 59,300 45,650	South
Ephraim (2:18)	An Ox (Deut. 33:17; Ezek. 1:10; Rev. 4:7).	Ephraim Manasseh Benjamin	40,500 32,200 35,400	West
Dan (2:25)	An Eagle (Ezek. 1:10; Rev. 4:7).	Dan Asher Naphtali	62,700 41,500 53,400	North
Levites (2:17)	An Altar (possibly)	Moses Aaron Merarites Gershonites Kohathites	 3,200 2,630 2,750	East North West South

In this arrangement we have a remarkable anticipation of Ezekiel's vision (see Ezekiel 1:10) and also of the four living creatures of Revelation 4:7.

The Camp of Israel, arranged and organized as a perfect square, foreshadows the New Jerusalem of the last day. (See Revelation 21:9–27.)

Order of the March

Chapter 10 gives the marching order of the camp.

Judah

Issachar

Zebulun

Gershonites

- Two wagons—Coverings and Curtains.
- Four wagons—Boards, Sockets, Pillars.

Merarites

- Pillars of Court

Reuben

Simeon

Gad

Kohathites

- Ark
- Altar of Incense
- Candlestick
- Table of Showbread
- Vessels of Sanctuary
- Brazen Altar

Ephraim

Manasseh

Benjamin

Dan

Asher

Naphtali

QUESTIONS FOR REVIEW

1. What aspect of God's character does Numbers reflect?
2. Why is this fourth Pentateuchal book called *Numbers?*
3. Who was its writer?
4. State the period covered by Numbers.
5. Summarize a few leading key thoughts.
6. Indicate a key verse.
7. What particular form does the book have?
8. What relation has the book to the rest of the Pentateuch?
9. What New Testament passage should we study along with the book?
10. Suggest a few unique features.
11. In what ways could you use the book typically?
12. How would you outline its thirty-six chapters?
13. What lessons can be learned from the periods covered by the book?

6

DEUTERONOMY: THE BOOK OF REVIEWS

INTRODUCTION

Deuteronomy is a remarkable and necessary book. It was a special favorite with the prophets and the Christ. It contains no new laws. There was urgent need of rehearsing the Sinai laws, seeing that the old generation, minus two men, had passed away. Each new generation must have the same laws taught them. The book contains the last words of the great lawgiver, Moses.

ITS TITLE

The Septuagint gives *Deuteronomion—Deuter,* "second"; *Nomos,* "law." Such a title was given, seeing that the book contains the repetition of the Law of Sinai. (See Deuteronomy 17:18.)

The Hebrew Bible gives this book the title of *Haddebarim*—a word meaning "These are the words," or shortly and simply, "Words." (See Deuteronomy 1:1.) Deuteronomy records the utterances of Moses.

Some of the Rabbis called it "The Book of Reproofs," seeing that it records the many rebuffs administered by Moses to the people.

Deuteronomy has also been named "The Book of Reviews." It is indeed a review of the past, with an eye to the future. It is a translation of Israel's redemptive history into living principles. It is not so much a history as a commentary.

ITS AUTHOR

Moses, without a doubt, is the author of Deuteronomy, as we can discover from the explicit statements in chapter 31:9, 24–27, and the "Song," 31:22. Such statements are either true or false. Deuteronomy is the handiwork of Moses, or else the book is a forgery. The above passages are ignored by higher critics. Moses, they say, no doubt gave utterance to many things that are written, but other hands penned the book some four hundred to five hundred years later. The declaration of Deuteronomy 1:1, however, leaves us in no doubt as to its Mosaic authorship.

Under this section we can bring together several unique features concerning Moses and his Book of Reviews.

1. His name occurs about forty times, and in the majority of cases as the authoritative author of the subject matter.

2. Moses uses the first person in Deuteronomy 1:16, 18; 3:21; 29:5. Such a fact indicates that if the book is not Mosaic, then it is a forgery and therefore not reliable.
3. Our Lord testified to Moses as being its author. (See Matthew 19:7–9, quoting Deuteronomy 24:1–4.)
4. 4. Deuteronomy is largely quoted by Old Testament prophets and New Testament apostles as the work of Moses. (It is quoted nearly one hundred times in the New Testament.)
5. 5. The reasons why Satan hates the book and uses critics to discredit it are fourfold:

It was the book used by Christ for Satan's defeat. (Compare Matthew 4:4 with Deuteronomy 8:3; Matthew 4:10 with Deuteronomy 6:13; Matthew 4:7 with Deuteronomy 6:16. Our Lord quoted it in the days of His childhood, youth, and manhood.)

It is the book that stoutly condemns spiritism (Deuteronomy 18:9–14). A necromancer is a seeker after the dead, a medium. Spiritism is Satan's great counterfeit of the day.

It is the book which declares the overthrow of Satan's power. Satan has power over death. (See Hebrews 2:14.) Satan contended with Michael over Moses' dead body. (See Jude 9.) God buried Moses and preserved him, thereby defying Satan. (See Deuteronomy 34:6; Matthew 17:3.) Satan desired possession of the body because likely he foreknew its resurrection and that Moses would probably be one of the two witnesses (see Revelation 11); so to possess his body would mean to frustrate God's purpose in the last days.

It is the book that insists upon the full obedience of God's people. The obedience and holiness of the redeemed occasion the devil's hatred.

ITS SCOPE

The book occupies the last days of the forty years' wandering in the wilderness. Compare chapter 1:3 with Joshua 4:19, and you have seventy days. Deduct thirty days' mourning for Moses (Deuteronomy 34:8), and you have forty days.

ITS KEYNOTE

The central thought is "Jehovah has chosen Israel; let Israel choose Jehovah." A further thought is "Faith in and obedience to God is the ground of blessing from God." Further, God's law is the outcome of His love, and His choice involves holiness.

ITS KEY WORDS

The words "commandments" and "statutes" occur more often in Deuteronomy than in any other book except the Psalms—"commandments" occurs one hundred times, "statutes," twenty-eight times. (See Deuteronomy 10:12–13.)

It would seem as if the whole book is a treatise on the subject of obedience. "Obey" and "do" occur some sixty times. "Hear" and "Harken" occur upwards of seventy times. God longed for the obedience of His people:

1. Because they were His own (1:10; 14:1, 2).
2. Because He loved them (4:37; 7:7).

3. Because He wished them well (4:1; 5:29).

"*The Lord our God*" is used about 300 times; "possession" sixty times; "remembrance" about eighteen times (remembrance was a motive to obedience, see Deuteronomy 5:15); "love" over twenty times. A motto for the book could well be, "All's love yet all's law."[18]

ITS PURPOSE

To induce the people to be faithful to the covenant which Jehovah made with them, and to prepare them as the chosen, redeemed, and disciplined people of God for entering, conquering, and possessing the land.

ITS LESSONS

1. The idea of the covenant, involving mutual duties and obligations, binding Jehovah to faithfulness and Israel to obedience, from motives of love and gratitude.
2. God's love demands human response.
3. Spiritual life is the basis of morality and social order.
4. Holiness is the standard of behavior.
5. Devotion to God is the rule of life.
6. In spiritual difficulty, remember history which can be read—His Story.
7. One sin can rob a man of the fullness of blessing.
8. The essence of true religion is found in chapter 10:12–13.

---

18. Robert Browning, "Saul" (1855), Part XVII, line 242.

9. Man does not live by bread alone. (See Deuteronomy 8:3.)
10. Prosperity tends to beget indifference. (See Deuteronomy 8:11–17.)
11. Chastisement, when it comes, is sent in fatherly love. (See Deuteronomy 8:5.)
12. Idolatry is a great foe. (See Deuteronomy 7:1–6; 13:1–5.)

ITS FORM

"It is the text of all prophecy; a manual of evangelical oratory; possessing 'all the warmth of a St. Bernard, the flaming zeal of a Savonarola, and the tender, gracious sympathy of a St. Francis of Assisi.'"[19] Its spirit is most ethical and religious. The tone is that of a father as well as that of a legislator. A spirit of humanity pervades the entire book. Holiness is its ideal.

ITS RELATION TO THE PENTATEUCH

It is the last of the Pentateuchal books, and its law and history are based on the preceding four. It is a fit conclusion to the Pentateuch.

Genesis: The origin of the nation and its religion—*Called*.

Exodus: The preparation of the nation for receiving the Law—*Redeemed*.

Leviticus: The ritual of its religion—*Sanctified*.

---

19. George L. Robinson, *Deuteronomy*, in James Orr, ed., vol. 2, *The International Standard Bible Encyclopedia* (Howard-Severance Company, 1915), 835.

Numbers: The organization of the nation for entering Canaan—*Conflict.*

Deuteronomy: The guidance of the nation in the land—*Blessing.*

Deuteronomy also comprises, condenses, and continues the great truths contained in the four previous books we have considered. For example:

The *divine election of Israel,* so prominent in Genesis, is here again emphasized. Israel is bidden to remember it, again and again, that by the remembrance she may be saved from the fatal sin of self-righteousness. She was taught that not for her greatness nor for her goodness did the Lord choose her, but simply because of His own good pleasure.

The *divine deliverance of Israel,* which is the principal theme of Exodus, is here recalled. She is bidden to remember what Jehovah did to Pharaoh and to all Egypt, when He delivered her from the house of bondage, that in gratitude for this deliverance she would find a motive for obedience.

The *divine holiness,* implying national holiness, which is the theme of Leviticus, is kept constantly in view in the book of Deuteronomy, and this holiness is constantly held up before the people as a standard which is to determine their conduct even in secular matters.

The *divine jealousy* and *divine determination* to be obeyed, which are so forcefully illustrated in Numbers, are emphasized with no less power by the awful threats of Deuteronomy.

The message, however, which Deuteronomy has made particularly its own is the message of *divine love and bounty.* Its appeal to Israel is, *"Thou shalt love the Lord thy God with all thy heart, and with all thy soul, and with all thy strength, and with all thy mind; and thy neighbor as thyself"* (Luke 10:27). Taken as a whole, the book is an exposition of this great commandment.

ITS CHARACTERISTICS

What a rich field of exposition there is for the diligent preacher to glean in! Talk about suggestions for sermons—this book is loaded with them.

1. The first reference in the Bible to the children of Belial is in Deuteronomy 13:13. "Belial" is a word denoting all that is wicked and worthless, hopeless as to character and destiny. The word is also used of Satan in 2 Corinthians 6:15.

2. It contains the prediction of the coming Christ, the Prophet. (Deuteronomy 18:15–19; see also Acts 3:22; 7:37; John 1:45; 6:14). Moses thus sets our Lord before Israel as the promised Messiah, a hope to gladden them and their children in the years to come.

3. We have the only other Old Testament reference to Moses' call (Exodus 3) in chapter 33:16.

4. The first reference to death by hanging on a tree is given in this book. (See Deuteronomy 21:22, 23; Galatians 3:13).

5. Paul adopts Moses' deep thoughts as recorded in chapter 30:11–14. (See Romans 10:5–11.)

6. Deuteronomy gives the essence of true religion. (See Deuteronomy 8:3, 5; 13:1–5; Matthew 4:4.)

7. The Law had to be inscribed on Mount Ebal (see Deuteronomy 11:26–29), the mount of the curse, for the end of the law is condemnation (see Galatians 3:10).

8. Its contents had to be memorized and ceaselessly repeated. (See Deuteronomy 6:4–9; 11:18–21.)

9. The book had to be read in the hearing of all the people every seven years. (See Deuteronomy 31:10–13.)

10. Special provision had to be made for the preservation of the book. (See Deuteronomy 31:24–26.)

11. We have the first mention of a bedstead, iron no less, in chapter 3:11. According to the calculation of some writers, it was thirteen and one-half feet long and six feet wide.

12. The book gives us the first promise of God's continual presence: for tribulation (see 4:30, 31); for the journey (see 31:1–6); for conflict (see Joshua 1:5–6). (See also 1 Chronicles 28:20; Hebrews 13:5, 6.)

13. The grace of God is glorified throughout the whole book. Grace is always the beginning of a true relationship with God. After this He looks for the true life by which the believer is in-lawed to Christ.

14. The emphasis of the book is on love which was to be the presiding genius of the Hebrew's life. (See Deuteronomy 6:5; 10:12). Moses speaks out of a warm heart and strives to kindle a warm response in the hearts of the people. The great motive in man is love, and love to God is expressed in obedience to His laws. Nothing but love will submit to the will of God.

15. God was an Undertaker. (See Deuteronomy 34:6). Jehovah buried Moses. This is said of no other. The typical

significance of this fact is that Moses represents the Law. Those who are in Christ are dead to the Law. (See Romans 6:2, 6–8; 7:1, 4–6.)

It is also essential to the typical meaning in the history of Israel that Moses should not cross the river Jordan, seeing that he represented the Law, which can never bring rest. It needs a Joshua, or "Jesus" as the name means, to bring God's people into Canaan's blessings. As for Moses, it was better for him to depart. He received something nobler far than an entrance into Canaan—a home with God and the departed worthies. Yet there is something sad about his departure. His lament at dying on the border of Canaan echoes throughout the book. "God buries His workmen but carries on His work."

16. Three feasts are enjoined (16:1–17):

The Passover is first, for the believer's relationship with God rests upon redemption. Pentecost, the Feast of Weeks, was the gathering of the firstfruits. The Feast of Tabernacles typifies the ingathering of the full harvest.

Taken together, these feasts typify a completed redemption, as follows:

The Passion of the Cross: Grief

The Coming of the Holy Spirit: Grace

The Final Triumph of the Coming King: Glory

For further typical suggestions one is urged to read Spurgeon's wise comments in his "Lectures" (First Series).

17. Like Genesis, the first book of the Pentateuch, Deuteronomy, the last book, contains a record of death at its

close. Moses died a lonely death, but it was a death with a vision, a death in the divine embrace. Dying, he looked upon:

A new generation and a new land, which he was not to enter at that time.

A new life, houses in place of tents, and a temple in place of the tabernacle.

New corn instead of manna; new duties to God and to one another.

A new leader and a new revelation for new tasks.

ITS ANALYSIS

From gathered material we select two outlines of Deuteronomy, both of which are comprehensive and instructive.

First Outline of Deuteronomy

1. *The Introduction* (1:1 to 3: 29).

    Incidents illustrating the Providence of God during the forty years' wanderings.

    A. Horeb to Kadesh—Ammonites not disturbed.

    B. Kadesh to Heshbon—Sihon sufers defeat.

    C. Heshbon to Beth-peor—Moses' request refused.

2. *Exhortations to Obedience* (4:1–40).

    A. Remember God's goodness, His sovereignty and absolute Godhead. He is the One and only God (1–8).

    B. Submit to His law and resist idolatry (9–24).

C. Should they lapse into idolatry and be exiled, yet God will not abandon them forever, and when they repent He will be merciful (28–40).

3. *Provision for the Manslayer* (4:41–43).

Three Cities of Refuge, namely: Bezer in the Wilderness; Ramoth in Gilead; and Golan in Bashan.

4. *Exposition of the Law* (4:44–28:68).

A. Repetition of the Decalogue (4:44–5:33). The covenant binds them to obedience.

B. Exhortation to be loyal (chapter 6). Their first duty is to love God, serve Him faithfully, and teach their children to do so.

C. Denunciation of fellowship with Canaanites (chapter 7). In their war against evil God will always help them.

D. Lessons from the past (chapters 8 to 11).

Remember the wilderness (chapter 8). Depend on God; do not forget the Giver while enjoying His gifts.

Beware of self-righteousness (9:1–10:11). From the first day they were willful and rebellious.

Give loving and ready obedience (10:12–11:32). This obedience to be prompted by the thought of God's favor, His deeds at the Exodus, and their dependence on Him.

E. Some special laws (12:1–26:19).

F. The blessing or the curse (chapters 27 and 28). Which? Choose well!

5. *Repetition of the Exhortations* (chapters 29 and 30).

A. Remember God's goodness and obey Him (29:1–9).

B. Privileges and responsibilities (29:10–29).

C. Repentance will bring restoration (30:1–10).

D. Life or Death are offered (30:11–20). Choose wisely!

6. *The Conclusion* (chapters 31 to 34).

A. Exhortation to the people and to Joshua.

B. Priests to read Law publicly every seven years.

C. Instructions to Joshua and Levites.

D. The Song of Moses.

E. Final commendation of the Law.

F. Moses commanded to ascend.

G. The blessing of Moses.

H. The death of Moses.

Second Outline of Deuteronomy

History, Past (1–4:43)	*Law, Present (4:44–26)*	*Prophecy, Future (27–34)*
Review of Israel's Wanderings and of God's Longsuffering	Repetition and Exposition of Law Given at Sinai, 39 Years Before	Revelation of God's Future Program for Israel. Record of Closing Events in Moses' Life.
Failure at Kadesh-barnea (chapter 1). Wanderings in Wilderness (chapters 2, 3). Exhortation to Obedience (chapter 4:1–40). Cities of Refuge (chapter 4:41–43).	Law at Sinai (chapters 5 to 11): Repeated (5:1–21). Expounded (5:22–11). Law of Religious Life (12–16:17). Law of National Life (16:18–20). Authority of Judges; Function of Priests. Law of Private and Social Life (chapters 21 to 26)— Home, Neighbors, World.	Ceremonies when entering Canaan (chapters 27, 28): Record (27:1–8); Curses (27:9–26); Blessings (chapter 28). Conditions of Covenant (chapters 29, 30): See Scofield Reference Bible. Closing Acts of Moses (chapters 31–34): His five charges: Israel (31:1–6). Joshua (31:7, 8, 23). Priests (31:9–13). From God (31:14–21). Record (31:24–29). His Song: Written and Taught (31:22–30). The Song Itself (chapter 32). His Blessing (chapter 33). His Death: Revealed (32:48–52). Experienced (chapter 34).
In this section Moses magnifies the grace of God. *"All things are of God"* (2 Corinthians 5:18). Does Israel possess the land? God gave it to her. Does Israel defeat her foes? God drives them out. Does Israel enjoy an exalted position? God has chosen her. So we have— A Unique God. A Unique People. A Unique Relationship.	*Please Note*: Four appeals to Israel make up the bulk of the book. Seven principles of obedience are set forth: The Fatherhood of God and His proprietorship in His people. The duty of separation unto Him and His service. Worship to be localized and centralized. All idolatrous relics to be destroyed. All idolatrous acts to be treated as treason against God and punished as capital crimes. All ethical relations to be regulated by God's law. The brotherhood of His people implied in the Fatherhood of God.	The secret of Moses' greatness was his wonderful dependence upon God.

QUESTIONS FOR REVIEW

1. Why was this Book of Reviews necessary?
2. Give a description of the titles of the book.
3. Can you prove if Moses wrote Deuteronomy? How?
4. Why have we satanic antagonism to the book?
5. Indicate the time covered by the book.
6. Suggest a central thought summarizing the book's message.
7. What key words would you select?
8. In a sentence or two, state the purpose of Deuteronomy.
9. What lessons does the book teach?
10. How does the book conclude the Pentateuch?
11. Outline several unique features of the book.
12. Submit a brief outline of the book.

ABOUT THE AUTHOR

When Dr. Herbert Lockyer (1886–1984) was first deciding on a career, he considered becoming an actor. Tall and well-spoken, he seemed a natural for the theater. But the Lord had something better in mind. Instead of the stage, God called Herbert to the pulpit, where, as a pastor, a Bible teacher, and the author of more than fifty books, he touched the hearts and lives of millions of people.

Dr. Lockyer held pastorates in Scotland and England for twenty-five years. As pastor of Leeds Road Baptist Church in Bradford, England, he became a leader in the Keswick Higher Life Movement, which emphasized the significance of living in the fullness of the Holy Spirit. This led to an invitation to speak at the Moody Bible Institute's fiftieth anniversary in 1936. His warm reception at that event led to his ministry in the United States. He received honorary degrees from both the Northwestern Evangelical Seminary and the International Academy in London.

In 1955, he returned to England, where he lived for many years. He then returned to the United States, where he spent the final years of his life in Colorado Springs, Colorado, with his son, the Rev. Herbert Lockyer Jr., a Presbyterian minister who eventually became his editor.